Coming

**POETS ON POETRY**

**David Lehman, General Editor**
**Donald Hall, Founding Editor**

*New titles*

John Ashbery, *Selected Prose*
Annie Finch, *The Body of Poetry*
Dana Gioia, *Barrier of a Common Language*
Paul Hoover, *Fables of Representation*
Philip Larkin, *Further Requirements*
Alice Notley, *Coming After*
William Stafford, *The Answers Are Inside the Mountains*
Richard Tillinghast, *Poetry and What Is Real*

*Recently published*

Thomas M. Disch, *The Castle of Perseverance*
Mark Jarman, *Body and Soul*
Philip Levine, *So Ask*
David Mura, *Song for Uncle Tom, Tonto, and Mr. Moto*
Karl Shapiro, *Essay on Rime*
Charles Simic, *The Metaphysician in the Dark*
Stephen Yenser, *A Boundless Field*

*Also available are collections by*

A. R. Ammons, Robert Bly, Philip Booth, Marianne Boruch,
Hayden Carruth, Amy Clampitt, Douglas Crase, Robert Creeley,
Donald Davie, Tess Gallagher, Linda Gregerson, Allen Grossman,
Thom Gunn, Rachel Hadas, John Haines, Donald Hall, Joy Harjo,
Robert Hayden, Edward Hirsch, Daniel Hoffman, Jonathan Holden,
John Hollander, Andrew Hudgins, Josephine Jacobsen, Galway Kinnell,
Mary Kinzie, Kenneth Koch, John Koethe, Yusef Komunyakaa,
Maxine Kumin, Martin Lammon (editor), Philip Larkin,
David Lehman, Philip Levine, Larry Levis, John Logan, William Logan,
William Matthews, William Meredith, Jane Miller, Carol Muske,
Geoffrey O'Brien, Gregory Orr, Alicia Suskin Ostriker, Ron Padgett,
Marge Piercy, Anne Sexton, Charles Simic, William Stafford,
Anne Stevenson, May Swenson, James Tate, Richard Tillinghast,
C. K. Williams, Alan Williamson, Charles Wright, and James Wright

*Alice Notley*

# Coming After

## ESSAYS ON POETRY

THE UNIVERSITY OF MICHIGAN PRESS

*Ann Arbor*

2008   2007   2006   2005      4   3   2   1

*A CIP catalog record for this book is available from the British Library.*

Library of Congress Cataloging-in-Publication Data

Notley, Alice, 1945–
    Coming after : essays on poetry / Alice Notley.
        p.      cm. — (Poets on poetry)
    ISBN 0-472-09859-4 (cloth : alk. paper) — ISBN 0-472-06859-8
(pbk. : alk. paper)
    1. American poetry—20th century—History and criticism.
    2. English poetry—20th century—History and criticism.
    3. Poetry—Authorship.   4. Poetry.   I. Title.   II. Series.
PS325.N68 2005
811'.509—dc22

                                                    2004025900

ISBN13 978-0-472-09859-0 (cloth)
ISBN13 978-0-472-06859-3 (paper)
ISBN13 978-0-472-02624-1 (electronic)

# Preface

These essays, reviews, talks were written during a ten-year period and, though often commissioned, to one of three purposes: to discuss a poet whose work hadn't been discussed much; to take up topics which seemed neglected or badly discussed; to explain what I was up to, since no one else seemed to be writing about me (a circumstance that is probably changing). I wanted to be clear, and not consciously innovative in language: I had done that before in discussing poetry and probably will do so again; but I didn't want to make, as much as to serve. However, I did want to invent a viewpoint *in each instance* according to what was required, that is, to see what was there without a predetermined terminology or logic getting in the way. Any contemporary poem or poet deserves to be approached without preconception. If it's of now, who knows what it is?

I was combating a climate of what I thought to be exactly preconception and jargon, the ways one is taught to read in school, the influence of critics and philosophers and writers one is told are great. Second-generation New York School figures, and certain poets connected to them through friendship, interests, publication outlets, were neglected, partly because they tended to disdain criticism as a form, thereby not creating a way of talking about their work (as others were doing); partly because they could seem anti-intellectual (as if a poet weren't by definition an intellectual); partly because their work was often humorous, ergo seemed "light"; partly because they tended to practice unsanctioned lifestyles; sometimes simply because they were humble or distracted, "non-careerist," which is not the same as not professional.

I discovered that, having kept in touch with the work of these poets over the course of thirty years, I could finally see what each had been, and was still, doing. I was impressed by how different each's life work was from the others' and with the extent to which each had kept faith with it—the work, the life, the poetry. And it really had taken me this long to see. Poetry takes time, and poets and their critics, especially, should beware of facile judgments (one hears them every day, makes them, revels in it). In no case among the essays about individuals did I end up writing what I had anticipated: I first thought to write about Lorenzo Thomas's poetic line, not his politics of the individual in society; I thought I would perhaps take on Ron Padgett's francophilia or humor, not his visionary qualities. Had all the time I'd taken with these poets previously been too unreflecting? Probably. I had been learning from them more than reflecting on them, seeing what they could do, as poets, as opposed to what I could. But essays finally get written so that someone does do the reflecting.

In the years I was writing these essays and slightly before, I myself had become involved in making poetry which had little in common, at least superficially, with the New York School or allied "schools." I was writing unfragmented epics, fictional narrative verse, in one instance a book which took a hard look at my own life and at "schools" (*Mysteries of Small Houses*), in another instance an almost misanthropic disavowal of all esthetic and cultural association (*Disobedience*). Nonetheless I deeply appreciated these other poetries. I still love poetry for itself: it strengthens, protects, and teaches me, because it isn't me. The pieces in which I explain my projects were partly meant to create a different way of speaking about poetry in order to make room for what I was doing. I felt slightly apologetic about changing—not that much but enough to try to explain myself to my friends. It's often "change or die": but one never says that, one says, "Poetry needs this next thing, which I will try to supply." My own lifelong project, as it seems today, August 3, 2001, has been twofold: to be a woman poet taking up as much literary space as any male poet, but most especially through poetry to discover The Truth. What else is there to do? (Answer: "FEED THE HUNGRY. HEAL THE SICK. RAISE THE DEAD." To quote Phil Whalen in "Minor Moralia.")

The book is divided into two sections, "Poets" and "Topics"; that is, first there are essays about individual poets and then essays about certain topics and my own poetry and concerns. The reader will find throughout the individual discussions of the poets' work an obsession with voice, sound, and measure, with political and spiritual stance often as a unified quality, and with the relation between the poetry and the poet's life or life-stance. In the essay "Steve," about Steve Carey, I was unable to separate his life and work at all and ended up making a dialogue of his biography and his poems. These obsessions seem to me to be both mine and the poets', though I don't think they would discuss their work in the way I have.

It is important that all of the poets dealt with at length live or lived in cities; if they moved to "the country" they did so after their voices had become intricately urbanized. I am that sort of poet too, and in that way I am always of the New York School and its friends: the Beats, Black Mountain, etc., the Language Poets, the Black Arts and Umbra poets, the Nuyoricans, the new-younger-poets-in-the-several-cities movement without a name. I love the city voice and hate what the city has become and how the world has become a city. Many of the poets discussed ask questions of the present becoming future, ask in their different ways: Where exactly is the world taking our voices and our lives? How can my poetry deal with the injustice and ugliness of the present? These questions loom behind the work of O'Hara, the "earlier" poet I discuss, but intensify in the work of Waldman, Thomas, Oliver, and myself. The title of the book, *Coming After,* refers to being "second-generation," and "postmodern," but it also refers to coming after an irrevocable point of damage.

Finally, I haven't included earlier pieces on Edwin Denby, Kenneth Koch and Tom Clark, Philip Whalen, and William Carlos Williams, because the style of that period of mine clashes too much with the style in this book. There is also the matter of all the people and books and topics I could have written about but didn't: but that fact makes a personal future.

# Contents

**Poets**

O'Hara in the Nineties                                    3
Joanne Kyger's Poetry                                    15
Ron Padgett's Visual Imagination                        27
Hollo's *Corvus*                                        41
Elmslie's *Routine Disruptions*                         52
Eileen Myles in Performance                             57
*A Certain Slant of Sunlight*                           67
*Iovis Omnia Plena*                                     83
Lorenzo Thomas: A Private Public Space                  95
Douglas Oliver's New York Poem                         108
Steve                                                  117

**Topics**

American Poetic Music at the Moment                    131
Voice                                                  147
Thinking and Poetry                                    158
Women and Poetry                                       167
The "Feminine" Epic                                    171

Acknowledgments                                        181

# Poets

*past the fear of life's paucity*
—Joanne Kyger, *All This Every Day*

# O'Hara in the Nineties

In 1984, a year after my husband Ted Berrigan had died, as I was preparing to teach a poetry workshop, I discovered a curious thing: that Frank O'Hara's poetry had frozen into art for me. It, like my own past, wasn't my life, a vivid motion-filled thing; it had died into artifact. The hatefulness of becoming art is, granted, one of O'Hara's themes ("the cancerous statue . . . / against my will / against my love / become art" ["In Memory of My Feelings"]), but I thought his poetry had outfoxed art. Now I had the strange (part of the "underwater" unreality of everything then) experience of walking into a class and announcing that the times of the masterpiece "A Step Away from Them" were officially dead and the poem now ice. Its late-fifties references to people and landmarks—the Times Square locale, the billboards and taxicabs, Pollock's death—had seemed the present for a long long time, much longer than they were "in real life," but now they were truly the past: the poem did not mirror the details of our contemporary reality, even though the billboards, some of them, were still there, the "lady in foxes on such a day" might still be there, and Giulietta Massina was then still alive. This was not our eighties detail—there was so much more to see that poetry had to catch up with; the poem seemed in that sense a period piece.

I stopped reading O'Hara's work after that for perhaps eight years. I scarcely thought about it, though it had previously constituted the most important poetic force in my life. It had been the poetry I studied and knew by heart and (confession no poet ever makes) measured my own against. Then in the fall of '92 I moved with Doug Oliver to Paris and began teaching workshops here. And this amazing thing happened, Frank unfroze. No one

---

From *Arshile,* no. 6 (1996).

From *Arshile,* no. 6 (1996).

knew his work here—no one knew anything much about American poetry, not Americans anyway—but no one knew O'Hara, and as I presented his poems in example again, the taxis began to move and honk, the sun got warm, and "A Step Away from Them" came back to life. As did all of *Lunch Poems.* I got to have them back, partly because I was out of the New York poetry milieu that had some years before used up both their techniques and presentation of subject, temporarily; and partly because enough time had gone by that a sense that these were of a time and use, everything is of a time and use that pass as we press on endlessly towards the so-called new form, new poem—who of us will be the winner of the ultimate progress prize, the genius-of-the-future award?—that sense in me had passed. Now I can see simply how good the poems are, how thoroughly they embody the experience of living and especially of loving in a world of fools, what a considerable scale they manage in such a small space, how well they solve the problem of voice and person and audience—there is always someone speaking and someone being spoken to or the Language Poets wouldn't list each other's names so assiduously in their essays, would they? Or to put it another way, who doesn't show off?

Here is the third stanza of the tripartite but entirely improvisatory "Poem" ("Khrushchev is coming on the right day!"):

> where does the evil of the year go
> >          when September takes New York
> and turns it into ozone stalagmites
> >               deposits of light
> >               so I get back up
> make coffee, and read François Villon, his life, so dark
> >     New York seems blinding and my tie is blowing up the street
> I wish it would blow off
> >               though it is cold and somewhat warms my neck
> as the train bears Khrushchev on to Pennsylvania Station
> >     and the light seems to be eternal
> >     and joy seems to be inexorable
> >     I am foolish enough always to find it in wind

We have here the syllable-perfect diction of the classical pianist's hand and ear, the dry air between syllables as between piano notes, wed to the unafraid speaking self, O'Hara's great construction: the interesting, direct, excessive, and/or plain voice trying to get at *it*—not at all the same thing as explaining yourself. The poem takes in the darkness of an inspired social outlaw (Villon), the tie-wearing anonymity of our poet, the historical occasion of Khrushchev's visit to New York, and in other parts of the poem a Puerto Rican cab driver's complaint as to Washington's lack of *politesse,* the Beckett/Ionesco Nobel Prize level of angst-stirring literary activity, a mother pushing a daughter on a swing, made-up figures from dreams, in short our world in a rather Shakespearian presentation of the operative strata of life. Home, government, art, the unconscious, in various social classes of manifestation. The above lines describe interstitial moments— reading, coffee, walking to work—and aver that joy is real, intense, with darkness and foolishness always hanging nearby in such a political world. Who is oneself then, these names, others, conversations? Partly, but you, the reader, are left with the enigma of the solitary person/poet, who speaks so intimately it's as if he were you, who know very well you aren't other people's names. But the century is your subject and you are its. What you have of your own, your self, is in "wind," ineffable poetry.

Frank O'Hara was the first poet I ever read who "sounded like me." Obviously he doesn't sound at all like me or most of the many people who've reacted similarly to his work: he was a gay man from Massachusetts born in 1926, I'm a straight woman from the Southwest born in 1945. But poetry is intimacy, it's an instantaneous transferral of mind, and this poet whom everyone uses the word "intimate" in relation to got right into my . . . the part of my head that has a silent tongue, and his waggled like mine. The first poem of his I would ever have read would be the first poem in *Lunch Poems,* "Music," whose first eight lines are as follows:

> If I rest for a moment near The Equestrian
> pausing for a liver sausage sandwich in the Mayflower Shoppe,
> that angel seems to be leading the horse into Bergdorf's
> and I am naked as a table cloth my nerves humming.
> Close to the fear of war and the stars which have disappeared.
> I have in my hands only 35¢, it's so meaningless to eat!
> and gusts of water spray over the basins of leaves
> like the hammers of a glass pianoforte.

Why one might identify with such speech feels obvious but not easily articulated; I'll try. One, and I seem to believe anyone, has a secret self, a rather delicately pondering inner person. Much of poetry exists to communicate with this entity. Its thoughts have the shape of speaking, but it doesn't have to explain as much to itself as one does to another person: it doesn't, e.g., think in prose-fiction sentences at all. It sees while it thinks, self-observes often, constructs scenarios of triumph out of utter vulnerability, etc., etc., that it melts in and out of. And it suddenly rather selflessly "understands." Ergo the above lines, projecting exactly such an entity, but why did they work for me? With O'Hara everything always leads back to the metrics. This is the sound of that inner music musing, a clear and attractive version of it, because if you order a "liver sausage sandwich"—and you do—you begin to think in a way in which you can say that to yourself, as if telling someone you ate it, your speaking/thinking voice accommodates it and attenuates, the sounds around it stretch out of it. It's funny, isn't it? It isn't literary, it's true though, and musical: "pausing for a liver sausage sandwich,"— that's me then. Once you've said that then you also say "naked as a table cloth," whose sounds contract in reaction to the liver sausage sandwich and the meaning of which makes you more extreme in comparison, naked, near an angel, or "close to the fear of war," which is a manly phrase. As "glass pianoforte" isn't. This poem is as complicated as a person. It isn't choosing one stance or attitude, as most poetry does, it's choosing several at once, in the way that my mind seems to work, but without making a stance out of multiplicity itself. The last thing an O'Hara poem is is stanceless. The stance is in the very existence of the voice in what I've called its fearlessness. Never afraid or hesitant to speak. Why shouldn't a "person" speak? The tyranny of Western civilization hasn't been imposed by poets, as much as we rail at each other to be careful; from the literary angle it's been imposed by those who make use of us, who choose, who compile lists and course plans, academies, universities, courts, editors, publishing houses, reading publics. Why shouldn't "I" speak?

One reason why the poem "Music" works, "still" works, is that the ear can't anticipate it, that's to say its music and phrasing are unique, don't fit any patterns you know—you may think they do but they don't. I speak confidently because once in a scary mental situation I decided I needed some courage, specifically falling asleep (don't ask why), and so resolved to memorize this poem nights in bed. I couldn't do it, I've still never been able to retain the first few lines for longer than a day. Thus it seems to me that the references of place and decade always come alive in the expansive tumult of the lines because they won't stay predictable musically and so refuse to be historical or sociological or local detail. "Mayflower Shoppe" keeps separating into "May" and "flower" and "Shop" and the unsounded "pe" and hovers, really, amid the first three lines: it's somewhere there when I try to memorize it, but where?

"Music" feels like a young man's poem with its "posturing." The slightly later "A Step Away from Them" uses its more profuse detail differently. The poem is filmic, a both warm and somber "realistic" walk played back at the typewriter. The detail *profuse* works as a monument to itself, the way that detail as sociology goes away in the great Renaissance paintings: first you think "she looks so Renaissance Italy in that bodice and necklace" and then you don't. Likewise "that's so fifties-Times-Square" and then it isn't. A third use of minute detail occurs in works like "Poem / *to Donald M. Allen*":

> and Allen and Peter can once again walk forth to visit
>     friends
> in the illuminated moonlight over the mists and towers
> having mistakenly thought that Bebe Daniels was in *I Cover
>     the Waterfront*
> instead of Claudette Colbert it has begun to rain softly and I
>     walk
> slowly thinking of becoming a stalk of asparagus for
>     Hallowe'en. . . .

Take by itself the line beginning "instead of Claudette"; it's jarring but true to the thought-and-life process—what's in your head, a movie star, isn't your raining or walking. Though "instead of" goes with the previous line really, but knocking this one gently makes a reality like thought and street. (It's not simply "Cubist.") Metrics, reference, and elliptical mental quickness fuse into a performance like life, not like a representation of it. This is the poem which ends:

```
                                              a knock on the door
           my heart your heart

                  my head and the strange reality of our flesh in
                        the rain
           so many parts of a strange existence independent but not
              searching in the night
                        nor in the morning when the rain has stopped
```

"So many parts of a strange existence," Bebe, Claudette, rain, and asparagus, united by poem, heart/head, which is always of its own times but reaches out of them by being committed to paper and voice in a precision of choices. The better the choices are, the longer the poem endures. What's better, what's that all about? Ear and eye, not having exactly the same one as everyone else, not the one everyone *says* is of the times, but just slightly to the side of that: who is Bebe Daniels? The superior quality of O'Hara's work seems also related to his character. I was in the first generation of poets to like O'Hara's poetry without having known him and been influenced by, almost more than his poetry, his character, apparently extraordinary in both its charm and what you might call moral force. So that the two qualities unite, which union, as I understand it, is the hallmark of the New York School. You don't try to say something without being worth knowing, and you aren't worth knowing unless you come off it so the person who wants to know you can be present too. Thus "my heart your heart," for that statement certainly spreads to the reader of the poem.

Rereading O'Hara's poetry now I'm struck by how politicized it is. In the past I had taken in the fact that it is often splenetic, but not to what an extent spleen is allied with a vision of a both attractive and hateful society. O'Hara's political or sociologic criticism seems omnipresent to me now: sometimes offered and then playfully retracted:

> I am ashamed of my century
> for being so entertaining
>
> —"Naphtha"

occasionally presented in a direct and rather emotionally ugly (why not? "Hate is only one of many responses") address:

We are tired of your tiresome imitations of Mayakovsky
we are tired
                of your dreary tourist ideas of our Negro selves
our selves are in far worse condition than the obviousness
of your color sense
                your general sense of Poughkeepsie is
a gaucherie no American poet would be guilty of in Tiflis
                —"Answer to Voznesensky & Evtushenko"

or the politics is a little ambiguous, or in a poem's speediness
hard to hold onto, or so much a "part of" something else, the
ostensible subject of the poem, that a reader might not identify
the politics as politics. I want to stress that for O'Hara it's a given
that one *is* politics, as one is anything else worth talking about,
in a whole way in combination with all the things one is, including metrics: "if you're going to buy a pair of pants you want
them to be tight enough so everyone will want to go to bed with
you" ("Personism: A Manifesto"). Art and life and politics don't
just conveniently separate out from each other so you can get
some easy answers for your new masterwork. But it's the metrics
that interests me again here, the relation of his extraordinarily
precise line to its content.

In "Image of the Buddha Preaching," the Buddha is making
a speech, in 1959, in the German arms-manufacturing city of
Essen, in a celebration of German-Indian friendship:

I am very happy to be here at the Villa Hügel
and Prime Minister Nehru has asked me to greet the people
    of Essen
and tell you how powerfully affected we in India
have been by Germany's lucidity and our concentration on
    archetypes
puts us in a class by ourself

This transnational friendship seems to involve "900 exhibits" of
Indian art; the middle of the poem praises German scholarship
in this field and then in a patteringly musical, stupefying (chant-
like?) passage, lists relevant materials and categories.

The poem ends as follows:

Nataraja dances on the dwarf
and unlike their fathers
Germany's highschool pupils love the mathematics

which is hopeful of a new delay in terror
I don't think

It's obviously the territory of the heavily ironic we're in, at least the poet is being ironic, but is the Buddha being ironic? The line "I don't think" floats away from the poem, away from the primary meaning it makes as an ending, that no there will be no new delay in terror. The reader remembers vaguely that nirvana is achieved in a willful cessation of thought. Perhaps O'Hara is also saying the Buddha fucking well ought to think at this point in history. The punchy conclusion is achieved as the culmination of a subject-specific "speech" delivered in a talky but formalized (public manners) line which can take in pomposities and technical jargon without losing its grace, then narrow into a quicker music and present that little flip at the end. When you think of "political poetry," you think of waves of emotion, bombast, indignation. You think of, actually, a politician speaking. This poem satirizes speech-making but fascinates by being deftly written, a poem; it's a demonstration of the sort of mixing of cultures, occasions, and ideals that has become, since the fifties, even more characteristic of our century.

The most famous of O'Hara's poems, "The Day Lady Died," can of course be read on a political level. All the details in it quietly add up to a portrait of white decadent affluence as opposed to Billie Holiday's art, life, and painful death. The opening reference is nothing if not political:

It is 12:20 in New York a Friday
three days after Bastille day, yes
it is 1959 and I go get a shoeshine

Where is the revolution, when a poet gets "a shoeshine," a process the reader pictures as a tableau of subjugation since the shiner kneels at the shinee's feet and was and is often black? The poet goes to the bank, ponders books to buy for his hosts in the moneyed Hamptons, purchases cartons of expensive imported cigarettes and imported liquor, in short indulges in a rather affected educated-bourgeois splurge punctuated by references to the "black world" ("the poets in Ghana"; *Les Nègres,* by Genet). This poem is more than an elegy or a piece of documentary, but its implacable metrics hold everything so much in place that my most persisting reaction to it is that it's an engraving or print, a piece of visual art, an arrangement of letters and numbers. It's a comparatively still poem, as say "For the Chinese New Year and For Bill Berkson" is not. The latter tumbles down the page so fast that the reader can scarcely keep up with the remarkable things it's saying:

> didn't you know we was all going to be Zen Buddhists after
> what we did you sure don't know much about war-guilt
> or nothing and the peach trees continued to rejoice around
> the prick which was for once authorized by our Congress
> though inactive what if it had turned out to be a volcano
> . . . . . . . . . . . . . . . . . . . . . . . . . . . . . . . . . . . . . . . .
> that's a mulatto of another nationality of marble
> . . . . . . . . . . . . . . . . . . . . . . . . . . . . . . . . . . .
> whither Lumumba whither oh whither Gauguin
> I have often tried to say goodbye to strange fantoms I
> read about in the newspapers
> . . . . . . . . . . . . . . . . . . . . . . .
> no there is no precedent of history no history nobody came
> before
> nobody will ever come before and nobody ever was that
> man

The five-line stanzas are relentless ("a . . . parade of Busby Berkleyites"), and few between-sentence breaths are taken. The poem is such a tangle of personal rage and public perception that you feel, after the hurricane's passed, you've been taught a profound lesson which won't keep still and which you must continue to internalize. And you like being yelled at in this case, because the tantrum's so entertaining (opposite of self-indulgent).

The pace of "For the Chinese New Year and For Bill Berkson" and of a poem such as the longer "Biotherm" strikes me as difficult to maintain. O'Hara's final set of poems, meant tentatively to be published under the title *The End of the Far West or the New York Amsterdam Set,* seems now to be an attempt to write at a different speed, possibly in order to write at all, since they appear at a time of significant slowdown. *The End of the Far West* is written under the obvious influence of Williams's variable foot, and also under the influence of television and its deadly flat diction. A new kind of voice is speaking, that of the poet becoming, and at the same time commenting on and changing, the story or issue on the screen. This voice is both satirical and mysterious; it's anonymous and communal (in the bad sense) in its exploitation of verbal mediocrity, and works somewhat more through deadpan presentation and juxtaposition than through intricate linguistic closework. For example, "Should We Legalize Abortion?" begins as follows:

> Now we have in our group a lot
> of unscrupulous
> doctors. As they do
> in any profession. Now
> (again) at the present time
> a rich person can
> always get an abortion
> they can fly to Japan
> or Sweden.

But it segues into other worlds:

> Strange . . .
> those eyes again!
> and they're radioactive!
> So stop thinking about how
> badly you're hurt . . . Stop coddling yourself. You can
> do something about all this and I'm here to help
> you do it! I'll start by getting your clothes off . . .

This is not a further foray into the land of the literary vernacular. It's a voyage into the more unpoetic version of the pondering self I discussed earlier. What if that one, that entity, does think in the clichés of television, has a pile of *these* units, these lines clattering around inside waiting for further use and rearrangement in rather empty contemporary situations? It's the space between sentences that's now remarkable and impeccable, but these poems aren't very pleasant, though maybe they shouldn't be. A warning shouldn't be pleasant, a pointing towards a future both inarticulate and full of words produced, re-cycled, and recombined by all sorts of machines.

O'Hara died two years after writing *The End of the Far West,* pro-ducing almost nothing in his last two years. I'm interested in these poems' negativity of outlook and their seeming voiding of what is now called authorial presence. It's not as if he's taking a stand against authorial presence, or is incapacitated in relation to it; it's more as if he would deny it to the world on the grounds of the world's incapacity to receive it. A sterile machinespeak is be-coming much more suitable for everyone. But also O'Hara's on automatic pilot, seeing where this language leads. His poetry had always in the past maintained its exquisite poise balancing life events and the language of the particular atop a secret self or cur-rent. This is the theme of "In Memory of My Feelings," written as O'Hara turned thirty in 1956:

> My quietness has a man in it, he is transparent
> and he carries me quietly, like a gondola, through the
> streets.
> He has several likenesses, like stars and years, like numerals.
> My quietness has a number of naked selves. . . .

And from the poem "Essay on Style," written in 1961:

> I was reflecting the other night meaning
> I was being reflected upon that Sheridan Square
> is remarkably beautiful. . . .

There seem to be at least two selves, the one reflected upon by time and times—the transparent carrier—and the one who might say aloud that Sheridan Square is beautiful. In *The End of the Far West* O'Hara is letting the underself take control. He's not willing the poems but allowing a new language to float into his primary area of operations.

Though O'Hara died young, his output feels complete to me, I think because he managed to get so much into individual poems. The poems from '59 to '61 especially are dense, not lin-guistically but rather experientially, indeed managing a trans-parence of texture while including so much of what's coming into a life at any one time. How did he do this? That's back to skill, sheer ability, plus a character or self that remains open to everything around it. I do still measure, sometimes, my own work, secretly, against his: he'll always be the better athlete. And I can find so much in his poems; whatever I'm thinking about or working on seems anticipated by his work. On the other hand, he is only one person, one of us. I want to communicate with other minds and—make no mistake about it—authorial presences. Or as Ted Berrigan said of O'Hara, "He couldn't write *my* poems. Only I can write them." Practically the most *important* thing O'Hara said he said in an essay, not in a poem: "The chair of poetry must remain empty, for poetry does not collaborate with society, but with life" ("About Zhivago and His Poems"). And one must leave one's favorites sometimes and contemplate "the 'latitude' of the stars."

# Joanne Kyger's Poetry

I first heard Joanne Kyger read her poetry in December of 1969 at somebody's house in Bolinas; it was the first contact I'd had with her poetry (I'd heard she was very "fast"), so I've never known her words apart from her voice. But I can't imagine any reader not hearing it: that her poetry is vocally sculpted is its most overwhelming characteristic. I mean that not all poetries are. There are some in which letters and words stand firm and dare the voice to make them give in: this is a nice masculine way to write; or there are uniquely voiced poets who pronounce/choose each word so carefully that one hears the voice of a playful but domineering general (Stein comes to mind), organizing the words into formation. In Kyger's poems the voice bends the words, but Voice is not a pseudonym for Emotion or Character, Voice is very close to being Voice. Here is a short light poem I remember her reading in that living room in 1969:

*Thursday, 13 November*

Unified School District.
    I'm still going to school.
                        Learning how
    to be personal    in the most elevated
        State of the Union
                        —from *All This Every Day*

The words don't separate. You have to attend to what is being said, you have to attend to a vocal movement which corresponds to a mental movement; the voice has charm, but though it says "I" intimately it isn't calling attention to a person. I also remember her reading the untitled short poem which ends with the

---

From *Arshile*, no. 5 (1995).

statement, "Whereas the real state is called golden / where things are exactly what they are." The "most elevated State of the Union" and the "golden" state may have been California, where we were; I remember we laughed, there were a lot of jokes about "states" at the time. However, these poems point to Kyger's major preoccupation, the attainment in quotidian life of that state where things and one are unveiled. If you think about it for a moment you realize her voice is the voice of that "search" or "state": not vatic not academic not showing-off, it is ordinary or actual life finding itself, which shouldn't be boring and in her poems never is.

Kyger's work from the early sixties, collected in *The Tapestry and the Web* and *Places to Go,* is imbued with Greek myth and classical allusions and has a rather darker feel to it than her work from the late sixties on, a progress that's the opposite of the usual one. Her early work is haunted by a problem of husbands and fathers, is rich but suggestive of revulsion, as well as being already casual, pliantly turned, and funny. Here are several lines from "The Pigs for Circe in May," in *Places to Go:*

> I like pigs. Cute feet, cute nose, and I think
>
> some spiritual value investing them. A man and his pig
>     together,
> rebalancing the pure in them, under each other's arms,
>     bathing,
> eating it.

There's girlish laughter and syntactical elegance and trickery, a mixed diction for a mixed experience, but another (untitled) poem from the same book is less patronizingly amused at being patronized by the established men in life and literature:

> They rise
> taking their way, the struggle of heads, walking
> strong and oblivious, with pomp and rich robes saying
> we are the minds of this country.

Kyger's work in subsequent books, though it most certainly contains lovers, subsists more in a broad air of friendship and community; classical allusions give way to allusions from Native American myths, as well as from Asian religions. Her poetry continues an involvement with narrative; the way her voice bends words is a clue to an involvement with telling as well as with thinking. She has a propensity for recounting stories in poetry, particularly recasting stories found in the course of reading prose. As she'd learned to use, really rather than tell, the story of Penelope and other Odyssean characters in her first two books, she now learns to tell, more straightforwardly, a Coast Miwok story or the life of the Indian religious figure Naropa. But one has a sense in all of her subsequent poetry of a wide golden light, which doesn't deny suffering but does contain it with constancy. Kyger's poetry is spiritual, natural, and transparent, full of that light.

What are the techniques for this light which is allowed in by a voice? The "I" of these poems rarely makes a character of itself; it presents its time or matter as what is seen, enacted, reflected upon, in unity:

> When I step through the door
> everything has changed. Finally,
>     it is out the door
>     past homes, down the trail
>     the lovely beach
>         draws me into her drawing. Finally
>
> I am past the fear of life's paucity.
> Green Angels, stream, in hot California
> and in the stillness seeds popping.
>       —Untitled, from *All This Every Day*

The margin must not be flush left or there is no movement, as in the walking and thinking in this voice. "When I step through the door / everything has changed," but there would be no change if "everything" weren't a little to the left of "when." And so on down the poem, to, for example, the unexpectedness of a verb after "beach," as "draws me into her drawing" makes waves slide down over sand. "I am past the fear of life's paucity" has been a peculiarly memorable line for me—"paucity" has the exact sound of its meaning here, an inspired word choice enhanced by being paired with "popping." The two words surround "Green Angels," letting the phrase stain them—for the reader a visionary experience.

Another poem from *All This Every Day,* again untitled as the
majority of the poems are with their "just-materialized" aura,
demonstrates the sinuosity of her sentences, the unexpectedness of their development, and their considerable precision.
The poet speaks of lighting incense before an image of Kannon
San, describes the image a bit, then says:

> I have read
> about her but can't remember
> it as really important
>
> for how she affects me
> as a dark little statue
> I make an intelligent
> pass at, when I bow
> I mean I am hopeful
> she evens off the demons.

There is consistent surprise from line to line, but it isn't just a
trick, it effects a release of passion, something that must be said
that contains a negative burden in conjunction with a hopeful
activity. For the poem becomes a putdown of "Holy Mary" and
also a statement of despair, terminating in a long period of un-
punctuated sentences:

> Oh Holy Mary
> you'll just say
> I'm not a good enough
> Christian
> to go to heaven &
> you look so sad
> You are merely human
> and wafted above us
> the Queen of a big
> church who staked out
> the real estate
> But then again what do I know
> of my heart but that it is tight
> and wishes to burst
> past the wall of my chest. . . .

The reader is still being surprised, but the feeling that has been
released by the technique of surprise is now much stronger than

the technique; the precision of "church who staked out / the real estate" is idiomatically cutting—a stabbing pair with "evens off the demons." The reality of the feeling here is obvious; Kyger always tells the truth.

An important poetry experience for me was hearing Kyger read the title sequence from *The Wonderful Focus of You* at St. Mark's Church in the late seventies. This event was held in the main sanctuary where one's voice echoed and traveled under eaves, and where a reader could look either preacherly or alone, standing near the pulpit. Kyger looked very solitary, performing poems about the lone self facing time and being cured of hurt and fear in time's process; she seemed alone with her voice, which as is characteristic with her, made unexpected turns and changes of both tone and pace rather than observing a consistent mood or metric. This reading seemed, and still seems to me, as deeply serious as a reading can be—which point I make to aver that it's not the bombastic or declamatory, or abstract or otherwise difficult, voice which presses deeply, it's the one committed to the truth. The truth tends to be something faced, rather than owned or explored: it doesn't always like you either, even when it can still be joked with and hung out with. A quiet voice is better then (in that circumstance), though quiet doesn't mean that quiet. Kyger has a lively, even extraordinarily quick mind-in-voice. It can shout too, even in this sequence, though not in order to dominate.

At the beginning of this sequence of dated diary-like entries we are presented with ideas of continuity and change as in the natural realm of plants with their seeds and cycles; in contrast the Human seems spiritually inelegant, desperate, shut out:

> Shabby Lady
>      You mixing up my time
> and changes of who I am and it's all
>
>           in the teeny trembling world
>                     —*February 15*

Kyger, I the poet, announces in *March 2* "The awful emptiness of you / who won't let me come to your heart." In this instance "you" may be Green Tara (Tibetan goddess of compassion— green as in the fertile world?) or the you in the poet's literal dreams: in other poems You, becoming "The Wonderful Focus of You," is "the Lord," perhaps community, a lover, nature, herself. Being drawn into You is to come alive again—after what death? A broken relationship is hinted at when the sequence is almost over:

> Say it brother, I want
> to be free
> and walk away
> from your smile and feel
> OK after while
>
> —*August 16*

But one of Kyger's unusual skills is to be able to be personal and not confessional: life is perpetual death and refocus upon You, the details are less in names than in the bite and color of experience-in-progress. *More on Thursday* ends:

> and I'm the kundalini snuggle that moves
> on the mount
> of baby fawn spots
> leap into the crazy arms of the impassionata
> utterly consumed

That is followed immediately by *August 1,* beginning "Bruised I am totally bruised full moon." We get change within setting, natural setting and emotional setting, and can identify without knowing more. Note in the passage from *More on Thursday* the layout that is the unfolding of each line in its own setting on the page, its own space—that layout is a voice making time interesting for You; time is lengthened cut slowed-down speeded-up, luxuriated in. One of the final conclusions Kyger arrives at is that "Time is a nice thing to go through" (*December 20*). But the very last entry is not so simply positive:

> Just sitting around smoking dope, drinking and telling
> stories,
> the news, making plans, analyzing, approaching the
> cessation
> of personality, the single personality understands its demise.
> Experience of the simultaneity of all human beings on this
> planet,

alive when you are alive. This seemingly inexhaustible sophistication of awareness becomes relentless and horrible, trapped. How am I ever going to learn enough to get out.

—"January 23, 1979"

In the *Up My Coast* section of the same volume Kyger, retelling a Coast Miwok myth, shows another part of her talent: for translating humor, and what you might call happy expressiveness, from another culture and time into our own:

> . . . Sun Woman kept on going.
> Come back! Coyote sent some people to get
> her back. She wouldn't come back. So
> Coyote sent enough men to bring her back
> whether she wanted to or not.

This is plain, so plain, as Native American storytelling often is; but the use of such phrases as "Come back!" and "whether she wanted to or not" is very skillful. They quicken and enliven the poem, making it idiomatic but not corny, trenchant. All of Kyger's effects in whatever poem seem spontaneous, and spontaneity adds edge, in fact, since it's difficult and everyone knows that, a real feat if maintained as a way of being or an ethic. This Coyote poem, which is untitled, is alive throughout with ordinary words used quickly, vividly, and musically:

> But Meadow Lark came
>                     and drove him away saying
>     People no good, People smell.
>                     When they die, they better stay dead.

It sounds like a Native American story and it sounds like Kyger; it's an example of keeping a story alive using poetry, the more economical genre, rather than the usual prose.

Kyger's most recent collection of poems, *Just Space, Poems 1979–1989,* is a logical follow-up to the struggle in the sequence *The Wonderful Focus of You,* being something like the journal of an arrived spirit, with a stake in a community of people and other natural beings. The word "journal" means "by day," which is how time passes, and it's time we're given to find out in, as "The Wonderful Focus of You" makes clear. Kyger accepts the quotidian, the people and events in her days, as the obvious ground for right living and less obviously for acquiring knowledge. In *Just Space* she has evolved a form of poem that contains more of name and event than before, but that is also more subtle and compact and quick in meaning than before.

*Just Space* is not presented as sequence except chronologically, but it is very much a book as well as a collection. It isn't laid out like a journal, but it's shaped as any journal is by the story time makes in a life, with people passing through, dying, being recalled, the seasons passing, wisdom being acquired and sometimes lost: all of that is a natural narrative. Any small town like Bolinas, where Kyger has continued to live since the sixties, as well mirrors the nation, so to keep track of one is to keep track of both. But notice how the book begins:

> You believe this stash of writing is "scholarly"?
> Out of this we deduce . . .
> From this we can see that . . .
>
> I know it's a detective story of passions,
> dinners, blood stuff around which the history of our lives
> crank.

The poem, which is untitled, becomes a disclaimer of modern disciplines—scholarly, historical—which try to make what's wild in us go away so we can be "in the know." One deduces ("Out of this we deduce," I'm afraid) that what's wild is what happens, and what happens is what this book is about to tell you. The book ends as follows:

> So, remembering to chronicle
> events economically
> and learning how to sit
>
> properly were what I thought important
> to learn from this space and respect
> and awe majestic old time news
> —"Death Valley Desert Notes"

*Just Space* works on a simple level as a Book of Pleasure, i.e., you can read it. For example, the gossip about people you don't know is quite biting:

Even Bisbee with the last stronghold of the
poor white hippies doesn't have such a determined bunch
of sleazos. Persephone Jones needs something to do
except being the Queen of Green Death & Smack. I arrived
to open the Bookstore at seven A.M. She's seated on the
steps. "Did you bring the Beer?" she said.
> —"Back from Bisbee: or Clean Up Time in Bolinas"

Natural description can be breathtaking, as in the following
complete poem:

> Defying gravity
>       the powerful serenity
>             of Redtail waits
>       to catch his snake mid wind
>       rain storm late morning
>                                          —Untitled

There is literary comment and record; the arrival of Language
Poetry, for example, is caught and both accepted and gently re-
pudiated as personal practice:

>                   The electric clock
> from the 30's childhood belongs to me. I am the I
> of this writing which indeed I like to do.
>                                          —Untitled

Note how in less than three lines she has managed to say she
is of her own time, to identify her time, to conjure up an actual clock in a room, to comment on the nature of her favored
first-person singular, and to suggest that she is surpassingly
content with the way she writes and not about to change for a
fashion. Language Poetry is also possibly the subject of the
poem "Yuppy Wittgensteins Arise!" but the poem moves too
quickly and subtly to let us know who it's putting down if that's
what it's doing:

>                   Gee glad you've got a horizon
>       to speak to You
>       are as humorous as the hospitality you enjoy
>       So you must go to the Dentist. . . .

Many of the poems are species of what we used to call the Clear Enigma: you know exactly what's going on, but you're not exactly sure of what else is going on. Elsewhere deaths are recorded, the moon rises often, people get pissed off at Kyger and she at them, she narrates sporadically the life of Naropa, books are read, marriages celebrated, animals and plants encountered. Phenomenology is a concentration on the outer world as phenomena appearing to a mind; and so Kyger is a phenomenologist, and hints that she is from time to time: one poem is called "Narrative as Attention on a Rainy Sunday's Phenomenology." She is more overtly a Buddhist, and her practice ornaments the poetry with references and more importantly provides the awareness of "space" in the title *Just Space*, the real background of the poems, the considerable expanse of white paper from which these shortish poems emerge, as the daily phenomena of Bolinas materialize and group into poem-forms. A poem on the death of the writer Richard Brautigan is eerily a good example of a public subject—and as such susceptible to scrutiny via whatever trite overview is handy—seen by Kyger through the details of real encounter. Brautigan, who committed suicide in '84, lived in Bolinas at the time. Here is Kyger's untitled poem:

> Self Loathing & Self Pity
> I finish Somerset Maugham's biography
> on almost empty Wharf Road Beach.
> —terrified, lonely, crazy, no religion, dies
> at 92.
> "I think a Tragedy has occurred"
> notes Charles Reeves as I give him a ride up Terrace
> as we pass Sheriff's vehicles in front of Richard Brautigan's
> in front of Richard Brautigan's house.  Well he's gone
>
> away, maybe
> a robbery . . .
>
> October 25

The comments on Maugham spread to the Brautigan death, which is caught in the moment exactly but exactly from the outside. Yet the conjunction in Kyger's mind of her reading and the registering of death makes a knot, an event, which also becomes itself, that poem. That poem is haunting because it finally resists being more than a shape in time; its emotional strength lies in that resistance, which is both the poem's form and its wisdom.

Kyger's "researches" lead her towards the end of the book to the conclusion that everything is the one thing, what she perceives, presumably the poem it becomes, and the infinite space it sounds out of:

> I'm not really used to God anymore
> Like is he any different
>         from that Flicker out there
>       flying & disappearing into the Broom
>                     —"February 1 Wednesday"

That's finally the meaning of her book.

When I began this essay I thought I wouldn't discuss Kyger's lineage and influences, the extent of her own influence, "poetry school" affiliations, and so on. I now think to, but here at the end and briefly. No poet is those things, and the poetry's the thing, as we all know; furthermore, such labeling by association is frequently detrimental to women poets. Poetry movements are generally manmade; women seen in the light of such movements always appear secondary. However, Kyger has a lovely poem in *Just Space* about her lineage, which I can quote in full:

> You know    when you write    poetry    you find
>    the architecture    of your lineage    your teachers
> like Robert Duncan for me    gave me some glue    for the heart
> Beats    which gave confidence
>                     and competition
>         to the    Images    of Perfection
>
>   . . . or as dinner approaches I become hasty
>         do I mean PERFECTION?
>                           September 17, 1986

Besides her connection to Duncan and to the Beats, Kyger is connected by style and personal relationships to the other Black Mountain Poets (Olson's essay "Projective Verse" is an avowed influence) and to the New York School Poets, particularly to the second-generation New York School. She is an exact contemporary of Ted Berrigan (both born in November 1934), another celebrated conversationalist. Being known as a glorious and fascinating talker can obscure the value of your work, at least during your lifetime. I certainly hope to have shown that Kyger's work lives up to her conversation, which I also know something about. Kyger's influence on my own practice—and on many other women's—has been considerable; she's one of the women who's shown me how to speak as myself, to be intelligent in the way I wish and am, rather than suiting the requirements of established intellectuality. Universities are frightfully conservative because they love their traditions and especially their language; idiomatic truth can't get born there, or anything that has to be new, not just wants to be.

Kyger was recently omitted from *Postmodern American Poetry: A Norton Anthology* (a very useful book except for the Omissions any anthology's prone to). One must assume this is at least partly because she's stayed away from the centers of Poetry's meager power; to wield power would be counter to the logic and even the technique of her poetry, would be for her a spiritually poor choice. But not calling attention to herself, she isn't always included. As her books show, her daily life involves, besides poetry, domestic chores, community service, local jobs in stores, frequent teaching at the Naropa Institute in Boulder, extensive trips to Mexico, and poetry reading trips to the East Coast. This is not at all an insular existence, but it somehow hasn't brought her the notice she deserves. A certain poetry isn't always fashionable. However each poet's poetry is, or should be, its own world; you cross borders, you get to know it, you read it being there, not bringing a lot of baggage from outside it, and it works. Poetry's supposed to be lived in, not assessed. This particular poetry world is green and blue and has a gold air fraught with a rather awesome but familiar intelligence—it seems to know you quite well. While I'm reading these poems I can't imagine reading any other; my own poems get stiff by comparison if I think of them. Hers isn't a huge output, but that doesn't seem to matter, nor the fact that hardly any of it seems long. It's exceedingly ambitious in its search for an exact spiritual truth and for the "true-to-life." The fact of such uncompromising truthfulness is as "major" as an epic poem might be.

# Ron Padgett's Visual Imagination

The words "image" and "imagery" are often used oddly or inaccurately in connection with contemporary American poetry. I think it is rarer than supposed for a reader to "see" something named in a poem: there is too much of sound and word going on. And how many times have people said to me, after a poetry reading, "I really liked some of your images," when I'd used none! "Images" meant "language" for those people, the complex of sound, reference, and meaning aroused by a complex diction. Furthermore the reader's mind is unpredictable, free, as to what it will see, reading a description in poetry. In a predominantly visual poem like Williams's "The Red Wheelbarrow," my own strongest visual impression is associated with the word "glazed" ("glazed with rain / water") and is of something rather indefinably white and patina-like but nowhere, or maybe on a red unboundaried surface, but like glue not like rain as it should be.

There is also a kind of visual poetry which uses imagination of scenes or actions which do not naturally occur or have not occurred/are not occurring, but being seen in the writer's mind are rendered in words: the freedom of the mind to see and associate a mix of word and picture is emphasized. If in Chaucer's "The Book of the Duchess" a "hert" is being hunted in a dream, the hert is both a deer and a heart ("herte"), brown and also red and also transparent, a human faculty, and John of Gaunt's heart, the white duchess herself; you can "see" it all at once. The difference between such a configuration and an occasion of surrealist "imagery" is that of different kinds of story or convention. In a poem by Reverdy ("Espace," in *Sources du vent*) the sky lies down on spines or thorns (*épines*) which are probably trees

---

Review of Ron Padgett's *New & Selected Poems* (Boston: David R. Godine, 1996). From *Arshile*, no. 9 (1998).

(pines? the *pin* in *épines*) and on its spine (also *épine*); you see a large ghostly back, with its ghostly spine, as well as the waiting pines like a fakir's bed. Chaucer's poem is a medieval dream-vision, Reverdy's is a modern . . . what? We don't call it anything, perhaps a daydream, which trivializes it sufficiently to remove it from serious consideration as an expression of a psychic faculty, the ability to have visions.

This essay is a consideration of Ron Padgett's *New & Selected Poems*. The essay will examine Padgett's work as a whole, but at its center is a 112-page volume of poems, with a cover by Joe Brainard featuring such images as a childish drawing of a house, cigarette butts, a cancelled stamp, a squarish biscuit-like "something," most strikingly the Disney dog Pluto with a speech balloon containing a question mark over his head. These are like the elements of a classic Padgett poem, which would be seen and combined in the poet's mind as here they float in a live beige space. These are Padgett-like images. And I intend to approach Padgett's poetry as a visionary poetry. It may be difficult to think of Padgett as a visionary since his work is so humorous, but then Chaucer's is too. Likewise I think of Padgett's work as extraordinarily musical, and various in its music; a quality which its bizarreness, its vision, might distract from if you weren't looking for it. Not all of Padgett's work is bizarre of course, a great deal of it seems to aspire to a frank normality, as in the widespread French polarization of the "*normal*" and the "*bizarre*." But my intention in this essay is to approach Padgett's poetry through its imagery and vision, not through its humor, music, or French influences, not this time.

"American Cowslip," the first poem in both *New & Selected Poems* and *The Big Something* (The Figures, 1989), both describes and is exemplary of an imaginative process, a train of imagery, which is at the same time an experience—"flight of fancy" in which you do fly—and a way of thinking:

> Nothing is
> the way you think it is
> going to be.
> Take this little flower
> from me, and let it go
> into the way you think of it.

And so it grows
and is the face
of Daisy the cow speaking,
she my young grandma
growing and wearing
a pink slip and who fell
from the sky that was
clear blue and pure
all over the place
you called home
as it moved out
from under you
in the slow
rotation of the sphere
you call a star,
a flower, a mind.

The pictures or images of the poem are initially generated by
the word "cowslip" in the title, the flower, never described as its
literal self, becoming the face of "Daisy the cow." The latter
phrase makes me think of the Bordens, cartoon cows used to ad-
vertize Borden's milk in the fifties: wasn't one of them a Daisy?
She had a curl on her forehead, long eyelashes, and a daisy near
her ear; I "see" her, but you might see simply a cow and perhaps
a daisy as she is named; then suddenly there are the lines "she
my young grandma / growing and wearing / a pink slip and
who fell / from the sky," which make one see a young perhaps
beautiful woman in a pink slip. But "slip," besides suggesting the
slipping and sliding of meanings in the poem, brings the
"cowslip" of the title back, and cowslips are yellow and starlike.
She fell from the sky—like a star? or a thought or a given, not
really like the cow who jumped over the moon, though that may
be seen too. The sky in those days was very blue, but home—
what you stood on or stood for, beneath it—moved away from
under your feet, in time, "in the slow / rotation of the sphere,"
which is not exactly the earth, though the earth perhaps is starlike, flowerlike, mindlike. One sees the curve of the earth
against the sky but feels the poet's mind rotating really. Every
line is a surprise, in a steady-paced succession of surprises, like
the rotation of the hands of a clock, or a procession of constellations through degrees of sidereal measurement. One is led to

"see" a great many things, but miraculously there is no feeling of confusion, because of the pacing, because of what is finally a sweetly grave tone, and because of the mild summery color scheme. You breathe and see summer in this poem.

In other examples of trains of images or quickly changing pictures, particularly in Padgett's earlier poems, the action may be funnier, more cartoon-like (his poetry often refers to cartoon characters and to conventions of drawn and animated cartoons), the leaps between "frames" a bit more breathtakingly steep. Take the following lines from "Ode to Stupidity" (originally printed in *Toujours L'Amour* [Sun, 1976]):

> You thought you would feel bad this morning
> And you do not but the street
> Looks chewed up, people lose their footing,
> Their mouths open in surprise as they slip and fall,
> Perhaps some old person will break their hip!
> So you examine the street, write a letter,
> Organize a march, run for Congress, lead
> A revolution, are stood before a firing squad
> Without a cigarette dangling between your lips!
> They didn't even give you a cigarette!
> No cigarette!!
> And as a final mockery to your ideals,
> The assassins are smoking four cigarettes each,
> Billows of smoke pouring from their faces,
> Vision obscured, so that when their rifles
> Expel the bullets, chickens
> Fall from the sky, 39 cents per pound!

Towards the end of this passage one is simply in the world of Bugs Bunny or Speedy Gonzales, the cartoonist has the freedom of the pen and isn't/musn't be limited by either the believable or the expected. The billows of smoke are very large in my mind's eye, though somewhat Cubist-looking with regular Léger-like curves, the chickens which fall from the sky have large tags dangling from them on which one reads "39¢/lb." Padgett's poems often seem to be about the journey they take: given where you begin, where will you end up? "Ode to Stupidity" begins with the word "Duh" and ends with the lines "Before he will sprout wings like Hermes', / And fly with his message through space and time." The poem's purpose is partly to become smarter, and the rapid trains of imagery speed the journey, show the speaker's mind speeding up and showing off, and afford much of the entertainment along the way.

In Padgett's earliest work the visual or visionary element seems only nascent if present at all, these works being language- or idea-generated, as a poet's early work often is. Some of the poems in *Great Balls of Fire* (Holt, Rinehart and Winston, 1969; Coffee House, 1990) are mistranslations from French poems, some are in an Ashbery-like "code," some are based on found works, some are transparent and clearly reasoned, some are collage-like in an open-field manner, etc. Though these poems don't use images to think with, their particular usage of opaque language points to a way of thinking that takes place below the surface of daily speech and its reasonings. Here is section 2 of the extraordinary long poem "Tone Arm" (originally in *Great Balls of Fire*):

> I used to know a song about a hamper
> It went
> "On a large sock, O . . ."
>
> The rind of Borneo
> Is absolutely zero zero
> An etude!
>
> Adjourn the cup is pure
>
> Is it perfect if I rip off your sandals
> And bring them to you
>
> A dress retreating
> Through a forest fire makes another whole sense
>
> Unfortunately and I'm sorry
> I forgot the star of the show
> I can see it all now

Although there are a number of concrete nouns in the section, I "see" perhaps only two things: vaguely, a figure in a burning forest; and also, because of the peculiar power of the word "on" in the third line, a sock caught under a clothes hamper. However, in this poem "hamper" may be less a reference to the object than to obstruction, by purity. The following, for me, is one reasoning path through this section: "On a large sock, O . . ." means there is a zero—the letter *o*—in or on the word "sock"— i.e., there is zero impact, the sock is hampered. "The rind of Borneo"—the word "Borneo"'s outer limit—is likewise *o* or zero, all of this an etude in *o*'s and an exercise in purity. No violence. But then, if "I rip off your sandals / And bring them to you," that's perfect too, a circular action, an *o*, even if it sounds less pure. But it's to bring you what you already own or know. The dress retreating through a forest fire is different but it's incomplete, "another whole" or hole or *o*, because "the star of the show," the woman in the dress, isn't there. "I can see it all now," but it didn't get written, and the person in question, the star, the real person or presence or issue, is in danger. Purity gets you nothing. Giving someone something they have or know is nothing. The progress of the section is from word to word, and each word is a topology, something to look at itself. The thought of the section arises gradually stepwise out of this journey through words; as in a poem like "American Cowslip" it arises out of a journey through pictures or a combination of words and pictures.

There are two interesting and complementary poems in Padgett's oeuvre, each of which focuses on a single "non-bizarre" picture. The first is "Poulain," from *Great Balls of Fire*:

> An orange and blue box of Poulain chocolates
> Is what I think of often
> As I sit just outside the late afternoon sunlight–
> I see it in another light
> Sitting on a brown oak or something table,
> Maybe a white kitchen one,
> And when I reach out for it
> My hand touches it
> And I pick it up

In this poem the reader doesn't "see" the box of chocolates really, the poet does, and indeed seems to be saying he's able also to feel it and even pick it up. This is to make a vast claim for the imagination, which I myself feel is justified: in the imagination the box is there, you pick it up, the reality of the imagined box is as puissant as the real one. The second poem is "Cherries / for Robert Herrick" in *Triangles in the Afternoon* (Sun, 1979):

Three cherries lie
on the mahogany
whose sheen deepens
deeper than the sky
inside the windows
light makes on cherries

.

I reach for one
but to return
my hand to where
it was before
and stare at them
until I am
here as long
as ever is

In this poem the reader sees or experiences deeply, as does the poet, the color and sheen of cherries simultaneously with the color and sheen of mahogany wood. But the cherries aren't to be eaten or even lifted up; they are too beautiful, too in touch with the sky, almost sacred, as the Herrickesque diction emphasizes: "but to return," "as long / as ever is." They are art and untouched become this poem, which lasts as long as ever is. Ron Padgett's great friend Ted Berrigan wrote, beside this poem in his copy of the book, the words "My Wish." I wish to see and experience this beauty and not harm it, and in my imagination wishing makes it so.

The wonder of, and the problem with, the imagination is that its well of images never dries up, as Padgett notes in the long poem "Cufflinks" (originally in *Triangles in the Afternoon*):

As for the unconscious, I have an inexhaustible source of
    images there.
                    Donald
Duck flies through the trees under a sky of exploding
    dirigibles.
"My goodness," he squawks, "what a hostile environment!"
    Etc.
I can tune in so precisely to my own thoughts
that they are in perfect focus, no fuzz,

but I cannot for the life of me trace them
all the way back to their origin. So for me
they appear from what appears to be nowhere, a point
of origin that in effect does not exist.
I would like very much to be able to go
back through that point and into

nuts? Maybe I'd go nuts!

I said "problem" above because it's hard to keep knowing what
to do with this constant change and novelty—it may become
tiresome, not new (I speak as a practitioner again here); furthermore one *does* want to know the origin of images and *does*
suspect that one might go nuts finding it out, disappear into
that origin, and one is already different enough from others in
being so in touch with the imagination. Also an imaginative
process that comes from so far inside can dispel the quotidian,
and that's partly why one seeks out the imagination in the first
place, but what about expressions of warm feeling, direct feeling, plain tonal transparence? Padgett tends to make a separate
genre of the latter occasions, often writing in prose then. I sense
in his work from the late seventies on a struggle with verse, as if
he associates it, in general, with the imagination and prose with
a different kind of truth, an emotional truth. His verse feels to
me deeper for this struggle; his prose is very elegant and clear
and still visually anchored:

> . . . When I finally located the gravesite of Wilhelm de
> Kostrowitsky, I stood there facing it. That wonderful pearly
> gray French light streamed down over everything. I looked
> at the crudely hewn headstone that looked out of place, still
> modern. Then, slowly, a soft image appeared on it, the
> image of a cross. A little shiver went over me when the
> image appeared, so lightly it was cut in the stone, and when
> I looked back down at the ground I saw Apollinaire tilt up
> toward me straight as a board. He drifted right up through
> the ground. I felt my heart give a little jump, but I wasn't
> afraid. . . .
> —"At Apollinaire's Tomb," from *The Big Something*

Do I believe Ron Padgett "saw" Apollinaire in such a way? Yes.
In a five-part poem called "How to Be a Woodpecker," pub-

lished both as a chapbook (Toothpaste Press, 1983) and in *The Big Something*, Padgett uses the "train of images" form to deal with problems of this his trademark method, as well as such issues as does one want to be a human being among others and like others. In part 1 the poet speaks of a wonderful sleep he once had in Florida:

> I had dropped
> off the deep edge of consciousness,
> here depicted as a cliff in big Montana,
> say. So tell me, O Virgil
> & Virgil "Fire" Trucks, what I am
> when I'm asleep, and my eyes are open.

The unconscious is beautiful, and one is truly awake and alive there. Part 2 begins with the words "I would rather not participate in this society anymore, hello" and seems to delineate the poet's becoming a "woodpecker" who "definitely will not participate in . . . woodpecker society." Part 3—these parts are quite short—features the comic-strip characters Dagwood and Blondie at night in sleep attire while it seems to be raining blood outside. Part 4 is about the phrase "film noir," and is in tone "noir" and gray and dreamlike. Part 5 is about the wish for, and the discovery of, a "funny place," which turns out to be this poem:

> The funny place I describe
> is the one found here, on this page.
> I had to leave it for a while,
> because I had stopped believing it.

"How to Be a Woodpecker" is a serious work about finding, in an unpleasant or questionable society, a funny place, in which one is a woodpecker, though not like other woodpeckers in woodpecker society—"peckerwoods"? One is, or he is, then most probably Woody Woodpecker, an icon of Padgett's one knows from another poem, "To Woody Woodpecker" (originally in *The Big Something*):

> I love you, Woody,
> when you peck
> on the head

of a bad person
and laugh and fly
away real fast,
speed lines
in the air
and clouds of invisible
dust dissipating. . . .

Woody Woodpecker is a trickster, like Coyote in Native American myths (and unlike Wile E. Coyote in the cartoons—Roadrunner is the trickster); but he serves the good since he pecks "on the head / of a bad person." He's fast and happy and loony and funny, the spirit of much of Padgett's poetry.

There are two short poems from *The Big Something* (also in *New & Selected Poems*) that I like very much and that work less by magic—conjuring—than by intention to say something specific and by deployment throughout of the intensity of that intention. The first is called "Dog":

The New York streets look nude and stupid
With Ted and Edwin no longer here
To light them up with their particularity
Of loving them and with intelligence
In some large sense of the word:
New York's lost some of its rough charm
And there's just no getting around it
By pretending the rest of us can somehow make up for it
Or that future generations will. I hear
A dog barking in the street and it's drizzling
At 6 A.M. and there's nothing warm
Or lovable or necessary about it, it's just
Some dog barking in some street somewhere.
I hate that dog.

The title itself is interesting, bare and short and suggesting that this poem may be a "dog," an inferior specimen not as good as the poems of Ted (Berrigan) or Edwin (Denby), both of whom died in July 1983. The poem's written in a sort of "generic" New York School style that Padgett has access to but uses sparingly and to specific purpose. The first line announces really an emptiness of image, and there's very little to see in this poem, there is rather an atmosphere and sounds: drizzling, barking. The poem concentrates on defining what is lost. I love the second through fifth lines, almost awkward but instead extremely specific: I like the way the "them"s and "their" aren't confusing though referring to different antecedents. The phrase "their particularity / of loving them" is especially good, meaning something about anyone (who are "Ted" and "Edwin"?) and anyone's contribution to a city or community missed when they have died. The long line beginning "By pretending" is so perfectly emphatic; it's the eighth line of a fourteen-line poem that isn't perhaps a real sonnet, but is sonnet-like in honor of Ted and Edwin, both known for their sonnets. The eighth line is where a sonnet traditionally changes, and so in the last six lines of the poem we finally get the "dog," an unpleasant or unenjoyable presence—how strange to end a poem with hatred of a dog! It feels even stranger than ending a poem with Glenda the chimpanzee turning somersaults in a cage (as in "First Drift," in the same volumes).

The other poem is simply called "Poem":

> When I am dead and gone
> they will say of me,
> "We never could figure out
> what he was talking about
> but it was clear that he
> understood very well
> that modernism is a branch
> that was cut off decades ago."
> Guess who said that.
> Mutt and Jeff
> who used to look so good
> in the comics.
> I especially liked their moustaches.
> And the sense in it
> that God is watching
> from some untelevised height,
> and sometimes
> throws himself on the ground.
> There is a tremendous impact,
> for the molecules of God
> are just tremendous.

This is a criticism of criticism that ends in an exceedingly unexpected way. The quotation projected into the future strikes me as accurate about some people's attitude towards Padgett now: that "we aren't going to bother to get it, maybe he's just being funny, but he certainly understands that modernism is dead and that he's an official postmodern." In the poem Mutt and Jeff are introduced only briefly as paradigms of the average mouthpiece; but then in a bit of pronominal sleight-of-hand, "And the sense in it," referring back to "that," the critical statement, "God" is introduced into the poem. For such critics God is watching, God has in fact dictated that modernism the branch be cut off—from where? Nowhere of course because there is no tree, there is no modernism, one might even suggest. But for critics there is both branch and God, who throws himself on the ground, creating a tremendous impact as of a critical or literary judgment, for "the molecules of God / are just tremendous," the smallest parts of the biggest thing must be bigger than any other thing, every bit of an important critical edict, every bit of jargon, every new term. There aren't really any images in this poem, nothing one really "sees," though there is a ghost of Padgett's picture-changing pyrotechnics in the way the poem moves. But one is left with a negative picture: what does God look like landing on the ground, what do his molecules look like? You can't see them but you see . . . something, a big something.

I have, for what is obviously the larger part of this essay, placed Padgett's poetry in a quasi-chronological, developmental framework. It's now time to say that the genius of Padgett's *New & Selected Poems* is to destroy any sense of a personal chronology. The new book presents sixty poems selected from a career of over thirty years, plus twenty-two new works, mostly prose poems, in an order that has nothing to do with time. For example, the first five poems were published, respectively, in 1989, 1979, 1995, 1995 (those two being "new"), and 1979. This sort of temporal disorder is observed throughout; there is no sense of a story. There are often silly or superficial links between poems: "Dog," which ends with the line "I hate that dog," is followed by "Cufflinks," with its first line "I am brother to the frankfurter"; two of the first five poems, "Getting Along" and "Talking to Vladimir Mayakovsky," are about walking; a poem called "Who and Each" is followed by one called "Yak and Yak"; "Wonderful Things," which ends with "Tell you wonderful things," is followed by "The Music Lesson," which begins "I would like to tell you a story. . . ." And so on. But the overall effect of this kind of presentation is to create space around the poems and force them to stand separately and on their own merits, like paintings in a gallery. You're not asked to share in Padgett's personal or esthetic evolution, you're asked to "look at" art. The visual phrase is appropriate since it implies the detachment this book partly calls for, the connoisseur's eye. Can the reader see that the following poem

### Haiku

First: five syllables
Second: seven syllables
Third: five syllables

belongs in the same selection as the long tour de force "Sweet Pea," which appears a few pages later? The one is perhaps not as "great" as the other, but as a slab on the wall, a work, it holds its own—fills the space it occupies, with meaning and design.

Intercut throughout the book so that one appears every few pages are the hitherto unpublished prose poems. They vary the sound of the book, create a design, and constantly, by being "new," in proximity to older poems bring the past into the present. They are all visions. Here is one, called "Alphonse Goes to the Pharmacy":

"For the third time, Alphonse, no, I will not go to the pharmacy with you tonight. You must obtain your powders and elixirs on your own, just as you must affix your peruke to your head each day on your own. I will neither go to the pharmacy with you nor affix your peruke. Not now, not ever."

Alphonse the miniature chihuahua did not suffer rejection easily. His big dark eyes expressed the full measure of the despondency he felt as he pushed his head into the little sombrero and turned for one last look at his mistress, then wended his way out the door.

At the moment I can't think of a more outrageous work by anyone. I suppose a critic (I'm not a critic) would say it works through juxtaposition, like a collage; but it really works through a sort of rough-riding: through the feeling of being rejected and tyrannized over, and a satire of that feeling; through words that begin with *p* and words that contain an *x;* through a sudden portrait of a dog who wears a hat. If nothing that the reader encounters in a poem is expected, can the reader be left with anything? Yes. This poem creates a strong emotional field, funny and scary, unified, like a Tom and Jerry cartoon drawn by Max Ernst using images from Hogarth. Others of the new works are similarly both funny and dark; some are about the imagination and seeing; one is about denying greatness, Lenin's for example ("My Coup"); there is a wonderful poem in verse about walking with Mayakovsky. They are strong and fascinating poems, new and old at the same time, since they fit so easily between Padgett's older works, yet feel difficult to talk about the way really new work does.

Padgett's work is unique in American poetry precisely in its fusion of novel imagery, humor that's based in both New York and his native Oklahoma, and a various musicality: who else has done that? His poems are weighty, meant, and superbly entertaining. His beautiful prose poems represent an effort to expand his articulative possibilities so that he will be able to continue to say what he knows. This is an original and important body of work, as a blurb might say, but one must sum up: Padgett has by this time produced an original and important body of work, at whose center is a manner of thinking based on the word as a fusion of all of its pictorial possibilities, both literal (how it looks on the page) and imaginative. This allows him a kind of access to the unconscious or soul or mysterium in which no meanings are blocked because they come from the "wrong kind" of diction. The quotidian, the popular, the literary are all present as they are in anyone's life and in words spoken now or dreamed now, as the figures in dreams are words but much more. Much more mysterious than words, the figures in dreams are funny, elegant, and changeable. We think with them every night, but Padgett also thinks with them in his funny, elegant, mercurial poems.

# Hollo's *Corvus*

*"le plus souvent il s'agit de tristesse"*
it is mostly a question of sadness      the trick's to
     remember
that *that* is absolutely *no* excuse to be boring
or humorless or too conveniently absent

    —Anselm Hollo, "Small Door at Far End"

Anselm Hollo's new book of poems, *Corvus,* is as "black" and sleek as the raven it's named for. Hollo, in life, always dresses in basic black, because that is simplifying, an intense, economical—minimalist—expression of taste. Hollo has said often in conversation, "I am a minimalist": he means no waste, no wake of garbage. The changes in his poetry over a long career have been more of mood and depth than of style, as if what is essential to poetry, once mastered in a suitable style, remains constant (faithful) in that style. The same style, or couple of styles, *should do.* The same body does, the same mind and the same voice. Hollo's reading voice is one of *the* voices of our poetry times, unforgettably deep and rich, capable of exquisite pacing. It bears no relation to a raven's call whatsoever; it haunts one's reading of *Corvus,* a book full of resonance across big space and time, big sadness and affection, since one of the things "minimalism" does traditionally is play to the void.

Hollo, however, is not inclined to a religion-based exploration of the scale of the cosmos. He is a skeptic, he says in "1991," probably akin to the unnamed "urban ironists" he refers to in "West Is Left on the Map." The vastness of space-time is seen not as godly but as what gets between the dead and the living, old times and new times, what separates and devours all

Review of Anselm Hollo's *Corvus* (Minneapolis: Coffee House Press, 1995). From *Sulfur,* no. 40 (Spring 1997).

humans and their cultures, humans and their cultures tending, especially in these times, to hasten the feast. Hollo is not just a cosmopolite: he is an internationalist, one of American poetry's few and so a treasure. The son of Finnish and German parents, he grew up mainly in Finland speaking Finnish, German, and Swedish. He came to America to stay in the late sixties by way of ten or so years in England and has since made much of his living as a translator into English from his childhood languages and from French. Thus *Corvus* is dense with a multiple heritage and with international relationships and interests and a sense of the special loss in time of a past in other countries.

*Corvus* is prefaced by an author's note on the title (Hollo's own name means "raven" in Hungarian and Finnish) and concluded by some seven pages of notes—an urban-ironist-"scholar's" framework. In between there are seven sections, most of which have been previously published on their own as chapbooks, the short book being dear to Hollo's minimalist sensibility and part of his process. Presented in roughly chronological order, they are all together a different thing from how they seemed singly; they are now a meditation on time and the times, which Hollo sees as unrelievedly medieval in the word's worst senses, and on Hollo's own past. The sequence of untitled poems/pages "1991" is an elegy for the author's sister, Irina Hollo, who died in that year in Finland. The poem is for the most part direct in tone and meaning:

> aye . . . past
> this bubble of assumed person
> glassy shapes of the dead *en la noche* drift
> beyond glad or sad
> fugitives
> from all personal referents

But it is interrupted towards the end by a long satirical footnote placing the poem in a mock historical perspective from the point of view of the future. Thus "1991" becomes similar to *Corvus*'s second section, "Some Greeks," a short set of translations from *The Greek Anthology* mostly on the theme of death. The two sections are made to seem both lost in time and contemporary. "Some Greeks" has a preface, i.e., more scholarly apparatus, which is in the author's personal voice but by its existence hints at the transformation of life into the rustle of the page in the scholar's hand. After "Some Greeks," "Blue Ceiling" and "West Is Left on the Map" are sequences of untitled poems/parts like "1991." "Blue Ceiling" is disjunctive and spacey within a sketchy logical structure, framed as the thoughts of a man reading *Harper's* while raccoons try to enter his house. The thinker/reader/writer in the chair—a paradigmatic narrator for much of Hollo's poetry—is entertained by such verbal mental events as:

> when you met him he was a man
>     now he is a postage stamp
>
> you can't open the window this is Dallas
>
>     "they took my billiard table!"
> Mary Queen of Scots complained in 1576
>
>     mice fall from the sky

These startling units point forward, in the book, to the explosively disjunct middle section, "Not a Form at All But a State of Mind." "West Is Left on the Map," which comes after "Blue Ceiling," is more straightforward, like much of *Corvus* ranging between outcry of prophecy—"and the shades they are a-massing / at the gates of ghostly Troy"—and expression of love—"with you, a thousand years would not be long enough." Time can't be long enough for love but is always long enough for war. Though there are ways of combating time: one can speak to Diogenes the Cynic in a dream; place oneself on record as a witness ("remember Bear's Head who . . . saw / when the flood subsided / only the white man remain"); read a cat-urine-stained book by some late urban ironists.

"Not a Form at All But a State of Mind," which is made up of six sequences, is an outburst of multiple voices in the sonnet form. These sonnets' most obvious inspiration is Ted Berrigan's book *The Sonnets,* in their use of quotation of others' and the author's own works, their repetition of lines, their Cubist fragmentation and remassing of fragments into new entities, and their reflection of what Hollo refers to in the notes as "aleatory numerical methods of selection." They don't sound at all like

Berrigan, except in "Lines from Ted: An Ars Poetica," a sequence made up of selections from a talk given by Berrigan at the Naropa Institute in 1982. That sequence stands out as "different," a blasting in of a dead friend's voice, in the midst of, in the surrounding sequences, a swirl of memory, opinion, song, and connection to past others, including Hollo's past selves. The section is preceded by, as epigraph, William Carlos Williams's statement that "the sonnet . . . is not a form at all but a state of mind. It is the . . . dialogue upon which much writing is founded: a statement then a rejoinder of a sort, perhaps a reply, perhaps a variant of the original—but a comeback of one sort or another." For Hollo the point has not been to write sonnets so much as to manifest a sort of consciousness, a mind thinking and remembering, consciousness being dialogic. These fourteen-liners provide an easily replicable container for what is otherwise formless and continuous though patterned. "Mind is shapely," as Allen Ginsberg says; but it isn't shaped like art. Hollo here is using the sonnet to place corners, sides, melody, further patterning on the mind's dense workings so that they can be looked at at all and essences extracted.

The first sonnet sequence, bearing the title of the whole section, is probably the prettiest and most classical. It makes use of material from Lewis Carroll, Robert Creeley, Jack Clarke, Piero Heliczer, Ted Berrigan, Cavalcanti, Joanne Kyger, Sir Thomas Wyatt, Edwin Denby, Petrarch, Jouni Inkala, Tom Raworth, Gunnar Harding, and the author:

> underground trees    slow darkness
> and fear has lien upon the heart of me
> magpie steals silver spoon    it is gone forever
> like the eyeglasses of the less fortunate
>
> in a terrifying gray light from the future
> the carnival continues    a place where a sad horde
> of such as love and whom love tortures
> point to the moon and break it

The second sequence, "Small Door at Far End," only four sonnets long, comments on recent twentieth-century artistic and critical practices:

time for your take, you assholes
. . . . . . . . . . . . . . . . . . . . . . . . .
a barrage of labyrinthine winks
. . . . . . . . . . . . . . . . . . . . . . . .
and the total Sargasso Sea of signifiers
they do my *research* for me

Next, "Lines from Ted: An Ars Poetica" is not necessarily Hollo's own "ars poetica" but is probably one that Hollo's mind often converses with and does partake of from time to time. Every line in this sequence has Berrigan's stamp:

I sometimes wonder
                    I sometimes think about how many poets
For example those poets in the universities with suitcoats on
Some of whose works I like very much nonetheless
How many of them broke their own hearts
Fighting against their own natural tempo and pace
          in order to try to write
What was supposedly the right tempo and pace
For English-American literature?

Hollo's line arrangement expertly corresponds to Berrigan's syntactical pace, his delight in making each clause a surprise and in making Byzantine thought processes slowly work themselves out. "Lines from Ted" is an absolutely novel work; uncategorizable as to author or genre, it slips out of any box one tries to fit it in. And so the sequences proceed, each with a slightly different shape and purpose. "Pterodactyls," the fourth one, is another short one, viciously political:

we better start digging our foxholes in the fourth dimension
& while we dig let us chant We Piss on the Serb Nation State
We Piss on the Croat Nation State     we piss and shit
on all your godforsaken states

The fifth sonnet sequence, "Villonelles," is a "translation," a much-condensed reworking of an older narrative sequence, "Or, to Hocus the Animals of the Pursuers by Changing Their Dream Cassettes (Old Thibetan Trick)." What was formerly a fifteen-page work in quatrains is now six sonnets, forming a mythic story which refuses to make sense in the way of the medieval past its characters, a dwarf and a queen, hint at, but is "sensible," can be sensed. Its qualities, and drift, are suggested by the sequence's last few lines:

> in the world to come     everything like it was
>
> in the world that was     yet everything quite changed
> narratives     disjunctive (yet) associative as dreams
> poems     sonorous     replete with handsome words
> while lacking all "sense" & "connection"
>
> the future world is sensible chaos     chaos squared
> or raised to the power of infinity

The final sonnet sequence, "Reviewing the Tape," is composed entirely of lines from Hollo's earlier large collection, *Sojourner Microcosms: Poems 1959–77.* The words of the past are summoned and shaped into a mysteriously allusive personal narrative of the past, ending with the following lines:

> the surface extends all the way out to the core
> wherever there is a hole distributed in space
> cave equals room equals window

There is no essential difference in substance between surface and core, so the usual perception of them can be reversed. In a context of contemplation of the past, this suggests that what happens and then has happened is a "superficial" narrative, something inside, while the core of the person is the outward one, functioning exactly now. "A hole distributed in space" might be the past, as well as being a room. "Cave" is one's unconscious; "room" is the conscious self; "window" is the world. Everything coincides. And that sort of coincidence is the effect of the sequence and of all the sonnet sequences taken together. Hollo's times and self have been exploded, turned inside out, and made altogether.

*Corvus* concludes with two ostensible collections of separate titled poems. "High Beam" is an expansion of a shorter chapbook by the same title. There are poems in several manners: the expansively narrative:

It was in his house I discovered
the monumentally baffling Ezra Pound
greenish photo of puffy-faced poet
on glossy black cover     & his better half Dr. Williams
                    —"Seven Years Short of a Hundred"

the beautifully *graven:*

                    calligrapher Berrigan
                    carved the Iowa rain

                                        —"Inhabited Eyes"

the broadly satirical:

                              but now
                    in these
                              "controlled circumstances"

                    they had, in fact, *become*
                    "controlled substances"

                                        —"Chicago"

Etc. Five of the twenty-eight poems are about war (the Gulf War
and the war in ex-Yugoslavia being within the section's time
frame); five more are elegies; many are love poems. The final
section of *Corvus,* "Survival Dancing," consisting of fourteen
poems, is really a sequence, unified in manner, mood, and motion—both broad impulse and pulse. The manner is telegraphic,
dense, generally pronounless:

                    toss coin choose stairs a door with home
                    black hole of childhood
                    upholstered in cobblestones
                    mystery & exactitude of human nostrils
                    —"In the Music Composed by Nutritious Algae"

The whole, with its beautiful title, is dedicated to "Sir Orfeo Joe,"
a.k.a. Joe Cardarelli, the poet and longtime friend of Hollo's
who died suddenly in 1994. The mood, again, is elegiac, time-
conscious, and fearful but rather playfully so. This set, and so the
book, ends with two poems which take an unsentimental stand
with "art":

art
loves
funny details

therefore is
a dreaming
& yes    joy!

elitist
for sure

                              —"& Time Trots By"


    yet she'll
    . . . . . . . .
    do art    eat well    never please wicked money

        always treat language like a dangerous toy
                              —"At Evenfall"


The above last line, the last line of the book, refers to a description by Ed Dorn of the snowy landscape of Finland, in association with Hollo's poetry sensibility: "It is so pure it treats English
like a toy" (from the afterword to *Sojourner Microcosms*). The in-
sertion here of the word "dangerous" is a rather (not entirely)
political act, since American English is now the most political,
therefore dangerous, language in the world; this change is probably the product of Hollo's meditative compositional process. A
minimalist thinks before (and after), as well as while, writing.
    In the author's note to *Sojourner Microcosms* (1977) Hollo
states, "more & more i begin to see it all as one continuous
poem"; and there is a constancy and continuance to his work
since which has born out the truth of that statement. In the
same preface he writes, "i seem to average circa 10–20 pages per
year," and one suspects that that is still roughly the case (though
the lowercase "I" is no longer the case). Part of Hollo's method
is to collect phrases and lines, which he meditates on and joins
together: he's the maker of the new object out of selections
from what goes on in the inner and outer theaters. A compulsive reader, rather than compulsive writer, he takes in whatever
words on whatever surfaces encountered, and he reads the
words that get said in conversation as well. Thus, cullings from
the world's verbiage, contemporary and past, constitute much

of his raw material, which gets mulled over, related to, and in general transformed. He's not a diarist, or a recorder of the timely process of his mind and world. The "one continuous poem" isn't at all linear, because an effect of "fashioning" a poem is to deform the kind of time we've been taught to live in. In "Blue March '91" (in "High Beam") Hollo states:

> the Species invented Time
> and probably Space
>
> its function to be their recorder
> until the End

But if art is a "dreaming" ("& Time Trots By"), it creates a different time and space as a dream does. That's how a poem is a place where a line lasts. *Corvus,* like all of Hollo's books, contains memorable lines and passages; the book is not a *text,* is much more artistically and spatially alive than that linear word implies with its origins in weaving. One reads Hollo to be in a different kind of time, as well as to make contact with a mature and responsible mind, which is pessimistic about the world and happy to be functioning, and which proposes wisdom, humor, and beauty as reasonable antidotes to evil.

Hollo's style is etched, compressed, and also compositional, meaning that because of the relations between a poem's pieces, the reader is constantly sent back into and all around inside the poem. The poem is never used up. The pieces are definitely pieces; take the following passage from "West Is Left on the Map":

> "dear chords of night: one is not rhymes
> but civil fur     come to bliss late"
>
> this creature called god
>        left one no ma
>
> boat sails into sun
>
> west
>        is left on the map
>
> an endless warble of dreams

The primary unit is the phrase not the word, and the initial, quoted couplet (which I take to be Hollo's, since there's no reference to it in the deliciously fussy note apparatus) is composed of four phrases rather harmoniously at odds with each other. Likewise the next couplet is two startling phrases, and so on, the phrases being units of both meaning and cadence. The meanings are quick and new; the cadences are terse but rich and have space around them, aren't at all jerky. There is also a more narrative manner, as on the page just previous to the above:

> the old man reached for a stick but the savage begged him
> in the name of all that was sacred
> not to hurt this snake
> saying it was
> one of his gods
> so the old man picked up a sturdy branch & killed the snake
> & told the savage:
> "when you said to me
> that this creature
> was your god
> you left me no choice but to kill it"

Here there are long lines and shorter phrases together, each quite distinct though the narrative is continuous: each is still a piece, marked by the reader with a curious pleasure that seems to take place in the mouth, even while reading silently. In both passages, there is an exact sense of prosodic unit connected with phrase or line, even though the unit is never consistent. Prosody, of course, is also about time; one may use it to go forward in many different ways. Hollo's way is to hold back while going forward: the future arrives slowly, the past is recalled easily, and the reader feels, in general, in the present.

There is probably nothing special about Hollo's methods, as outlined; there is probably nothing very special about any poet's methods. However, it's difficult to think of anyone who practices the same methods as Hollo, anyone who gets meanings in quite the same way. He doesn't join the disjunct, he doesn't change syntax; rather by being terse, and careful, he brings things together that come to belong together.

It's the space between "pieces" that's important, different, space meaning a sort of register of the singularity of what's said. In disjunction it's the place where one recognizes that the next unit doesn't "go with" the previous one. Often in contemporary disjunction, the space between units is a mannerism (not necessarily a pejorative word), an element of design or style. In Hollo's writing, since there's content, such space exists because original thoughts are being uttered. But they're word-thoughts, thoughts that couldn't quite be had apart from the exact words they are. Somewhat the same kind of space exists between the poems or parts of the various chapbook-like sections of *Corvus,* between the sections themselves, and between all of Hollo's books. They—the various parts of the "one continuous thing," Hollo's lifelong poem—are of the same substance but aren't the same. They aren't novel: the aesthetics of novelty can be very wearying and shallow. They're an exact response to what's going on. Hollo's style opens to a large range of subject, since it is at once personal, magisterial, humorous, and serious. It compresses many qualities into the one response, in slow forward motion, with slow jewel-tipped feelers. Hollo's particular mastery of the space in and around the various units involved in the lifelong production of poetry, his particular practice, is probably closest, among contemporaries, to that of Ted Berrigan. Space in a poem is a frame both formal and friendly; it's a person-made tinkering with time. One does not become grandiose about such things; poetics doesn't change the world much, or shouldn't. (Wouldn't it be terrible if a poet actually changed the world's consciousness to be like her/his theory, or poem!) Or, as Hollo says in "Blue Ceiling," "may you be forever strange."

Finally, if Hollo is an internationalist, what is an international poetry? Sometimes it seems as if every American poet should be asking her/himself that question, as a response both to the United States' continuously imperialistic role in the world in most respects (including poetry) and to the fact of a borderless computer-controlled future. Hollo's poetry is faithful to ethnic region as well as to world, to a childhood in Finland that isn't really lost, and to various localities lived in in the American West. Specific histories don't fade, but one keeps in constant touch, outward. Hollo's poetry, with its huge field of reference, is one possible model for the future. It doesn't list what it knows and consists of: the references are built in. That is, it isn't itself a computerized conglomerate, doesn't spout facts as possession, but it's equal to all that. It could probably handle the future.

# Elmslie's *Routine Disruptions*

Contemplating writing this review of *Routine Disruptions: Selected Poems & Lyrics* by Kenward Elmslie—an excellent collection—I've been unable to dislodge a picture from my mind. It is of Elmslie during a reading several years ago, with a large "hat" on, made by an artist, that used as its primary image a large brassiere. A man reading poetry with a brassiere on his head! This is an icon, for me, of Elmslie's work, its wild funniness, theatricality, brazenness, its love of art and objects. Cleanly designed strange or beautiful objects, as in poems, as poems, words as objects, but . . . this is not a doctrine, and the face below the bra-hat, Kenward Elmslie's pleased bemused own, never disappears. Disruptions, as the title says, things never being the way they're supposed to be, stories never turning out the way they're supposed to. Upset expectations. Gender upsets, but isn't the idea of "gender" rather mild compared to the wearing of this hat? It isn't gender, it's the gratuity of everything we participate in, as invented, e.g., the wearing of hats; it's also the gratuity of life's real givens, its natural forms—heads and breasts are weird. Elmslie has never done what he was supposed to, and after the nearly forty years this book represents, his poetry can be seen to be unique. You do keep reading the poems, not because they're part of an ongoing discussion as to What Poetry Should Be Right Now, but because they continue to be unpredictable and unlike (other poetry) and lifelike (weird, patterned, tender).

Much of Elmslie's work has been in the form of librettos and lyrics, words for songs. Thus two things might be mentioned: a

Review of Kenward Elmslie's *Routine Disruptions: Selected Poems & Lyrics* (Minneapolis: Coffee House Press, 1998). From *Poetry Project Newsletter,* no. 173 (February–March 1999).

sense of a poem as not so much a drama as a small theater, with a stage to be enlivened; and a sound/metric influenced by popular song (as well as by something Beat-poetry-like, in that use of the articleless pronounless word pileup characteristic of people born in the twenties).

When I say an Elmslie poem may be theatrical I mean that people, objects, and words themselves often seem to be onstage or perhaps on a psychic stage, lit in any of the varieties of stage lightings, not just spotlit. The poet makes a speech, or the poet is in a setting, or the poet himself isn't the poem this time; but there is a distance involved, which isn't impersonal but full of regard—looking—and the desire to make something happen. What happens emerges from the singular imagination of Elmslie, or out of words themselves coming alive and making things happen:

> and I've been traveling ever since,
> so let's go find an open glade
> like the ones in sporting prints,
> (betrayed, delayed, afraid)
>
> where we'll lie among the air-plants
> in a perfect amphitheater in a soft pink afterglow.
> How those handsome birds can prance,
> ah . . . unattainable tableau.
>
> Let's scratch the ground clean,
> remove all stones and trash,
> I mean open dance halls in the forest, I mean
> where the earth's packed smooth and hard. Crash.
>
> It's the Tale of the Creation. The whip cracks.
> —"Feathered Dancers"

Ché is so trusting re "Truth and Consequences." Too Yanquified. He has dreams of pressing flesh with Nixon in native village. They go in one, light toke, just sit there. Pow! Nixon is converted! He brings the brass, light toke. They're converted! Big Ten Day Speech to the U.S.A. Must stop "exploiting" etc. Impeached, natch. Chaos! Village? Corpse smoke rises from distant chimney. Bumblebees crawling around the empty Bumblebee tuna can.
—"Tropicalism"

Kinky gentry into ransom crud used up.
Holding our own in flustery weather used up.
Many restful oases here in Hat City,
same old snappy salutes at the roadblocks
where om-like hum of shoot-out traffic
of scant interest to us fine-eared hold-outs,
honed to love outcries in the painted desert,
shrieks from humanoid wind tunnels.

—"Communications Equipment"

Notice how the references to Ché and Nixon have not dated; persons and things in such a "light" are not in time. As for the songlike metric, I can hear it throughout the book. Further I find it hard to distinguish "songs" from "poems," since Elmslie has achieved the Campionesque feat of writing songs which are also exactly poems on the page; they often have fancy, page-oriented layouts. "Bio" is classified as a "poem song" in the "Poem Songs" section:

Never saw "action"              ransacked my dance act
Came up with                        a nance act

        Trek            aids
        Sped up the decades

        Loved            ones
        Re-re-re-re-re-re-re-reruns

On the page it looks a bit like concrete poetry. "Girl Machine," which was also set to music, looks a *lot* like concrete poetry. A more "ordinary" song like "Brazil" (with the refrain "No extra-dition! Nya Nya Nya Nya Nya"), which is included in a section entitled "Song Lyrics I," displays the repetitions that song ordinarily includes and which permeate Elmslie's works called "poems." A work called "Kitchen," which is ostensibly a prose poem and which is composed of paragraphs designed to accompany black-and-white artwork by Joe Brainard, also sounds like an Elmslie song:

The faucetry demo has 4 4 × 4s. Subtexts. Food Love. It's a Moviola. Sex Love. Paired up like wed. Money Love. Moviola. ?eat? TV gameshow veer, Vanna batwings on roller-skates, humps the pristine blanks. Lingo frottage. Th, tire-chain, on wintry country lane, her first diphthong. Th. Th. Th. DeathLove, you big lummox! Th. Th. DeathLove Moviola 4 × 4.

Experience becomes songlike, also patterned, both at once, aural and visual, though one of Elmslie's poem titles, "Visual Radios," also suggests the overall effect of his works. Something you hear and see but finally you hear more than see, because that's what poetry's like, it occurs between words where their sounds meet. A songwriter usually works on the premise that the "music" takes care of the between-words part; a poet can't. Elmslie is a poet in both forms, poetry and lyrics.

As for the Elmslie narrative, here is the plot summary of a poem called "Japanese City." It is Melville's centennial so there is an appropriate celebration in that priests(!) release whale balloons, there are whale floats, etc. (Where are we?) "I" is in a hotel room and phones room service for ice water. There are cattle in the streets. (Cattle?) A Mexican seamstress keeps bringing I's clothes to him because he sweats a lot. (Is he in Mexico?) She tells him about some green caves which are cool. Description of the "other travelers'" hairs around the washbasin, what these hairs smell like. (Hairs? Hairs' smells?) Suddenly Jim the Salesman and his friends are massaging I's feet. Jim plays a card game and there is reference to (is it the card game?) red even numbers and green even numbers (no odd numbers) and their associations(!). Talk. About fish hatcheries and a disease one contracts from working in them called "the gills"(!). Ice water. Speculations about the evening. More Melville celebration. Jim and his friends leave. What does this tropical story have to do with the title, which refers to a very large construction by Joe Brainard, called *Japanese City,* that fell apart after approximately two years? I'm not sure. Elmslie never spells out his connections; they aren't really bizarre but are unexpected because of lack of conventional transition: "but mine, how perverse! Form a hoop, you there. Mine, / mine smell like old apples in a drawer. Jim the Salesman / and his cohorts are massaging my feet: a real treadmill example." The "mine" refers to the hairs around the washbasin, and it's quite possible that the earlier word "washbasin" has triggered the words "Jim the Salesman" and that's how Jim gets to be there, and so suddenly, for that's the first mention of him, midline as if we must have expected it. In an Elmslie fiction I can never figure out how much to "believe," I mean was Elmslie once, at least, in a room in, say, Mexico? I don't know. I like not knowing. Why? I don't know. And not knowing feels more profound than knowing.

Behind all this invention the personal Kenward looms, and he sometimes shows himself quite nakedly. Works that relate to Joe Brainard, Elmslie's longtime lover, partner, collaborator until Brainard's death in 1994, are especially revelatory. Elmslie's "One Hundred I Remembers," inspired by Brainard's book-length work *I Remember,* is extraordinary even though he didn't invent the form (any good form can be reused, that's what it's for). "I Remember my father, in the middle of the night, waking me up to tell me my mother had died. The last thing she told him, so he said, was *Be Kind.* For a long time this stuck in my mind, as if it were an admonition of gigantic importance that applied to me too." "I Remember shitting, and very tiny gold balls began racing around the blue linoleum bathroom floor. Then suddenly they stopped and vanished. I never saw them again, much to my relief, for there was no 'rational explanation' for them."

"Bare Bones," an account of Elmslie's life with Brainard, is what the title implies, a plain honest narrative, but also it implies the physical starkness of death from AIDS, described with a tact equal to Brainard's own. "Bare Bones" is preceded here by the violent "Champ Dust," quite a contrast. They are the two longest pieces in the last section, "Poems 1991–98" and make it a very powerful section. Such power implies future promise, even with sorrow around and even after so many years. The last poem in the book is called "Happy Re-Return" and ends in a deeply satisfying insouciance:

> Me, um, no deadbeat despite laughing stock enjambments.
> I did pay for my own sieve hoax, traumatized awful, by La Boo.
> Diaphanous Frenchie swamp goo-goo Gods curl me up fatal.
> Die alone. Orphan fate, whomped. I meant: curl me up fetal.
> How to downsize as co-waifs. Swing and sway and we'll do OK,
> Light years apart. Inches away—the schtick of eons,
> Afflatus deconstructed. Postmoderns, besnouted, gaze at us.
> Rest in peace, shitheads. Springtime births great bone decor.

# Eileen Myles in Performance

"I don't make up much," Eileen Myles says in her essay "How I Wrote Certain Of My Poems." "I don't think most poets do." *Now this isn't true,* is my reaction. The fact is that many poets do "make things up," practice the art of imagination inventing figures and stories for example, as well as the form of the poem, Myles's chosen focus. Myles perpetually reinvents form as a curious fluidity: she imagines her way through each of her poems as if there were always a new path through a familiar but ever-dangerous landscape. Her poems consist of the path and the person who follows it, not so much the landscape—New York City's East Village, which is well-known in the poems of others and in general well-known:

> I am filled
> with the death
> of the streets,
> you've seen me before—
> you're a wit-
> ness to the
> death of
> my innocence. . . .
> —"Hot Night," from *Not Me*

In this poetry, the question is "Who's walking there?" And so it is appropriate to begin writing about her with a quibble (whether or not poets make things up), since her poetry is so enclosed around the who of it, naturally inviting argument. I don't intend to argue really, I'm just pointing out the possibility. Myles's poetry presents a pretty naked self, lays self on the line: so there's always the possibility of the reader's reacting to this work as if it

From *Talisman,* no. 17 (Summer 1997).

were a person to be loved or liked or disagreed with or found obnoxious. The work is quite different from O'Hara's or Berrigan's. The former was never so classical as when supposedly being most personal—what is the love in *Love Poems (Tentative Title)* if not that for the poem itself? And who is doing the loving, not a person, a poet. Ted Berrigan was most often engaged in placing elements of the inner and outer consciousness into composition with each other, in order to make something unlike its elements. Myles's total project is, simply and grandly, the person herself as life and poem, style and content:

> Life is a plot to make me move.
> I fill its forms, an unwitting
> crayon
>
> I am prey to the materials
> of me, combinations
> create me into something
> else, civilization's inventions
>
> numb me, placate me
> carry me around.
> —"The Irony of the Leash," from *Maxfield Parrish*

Eileen Myles's work is heroic, monolithic, pure. The outward forms may vary, but the self at their center is constant; to maintain a stance for such a long time is courageous. Really the work hasn't changed much over the years, since she realized what its nature would be, in the seventies, in the books *A Fresh Young Voice from the Plains* and *Sappho's Boat*. The shape of the later longer poems in *Not Me* and *Maxfield Parrish: Early & New Poems* is already essentially realized in early poems such as "The Irony of the Leash" and "Romantic Pain," though she had not yet met James Schuyler and achieved her footlike short line, responding to but different from his own chiseled one. Hers pushes ahead into a long prose-sounding utterance, a longer "line" which comprises whole sentences (the whole utterance is more like the line than the lines are):

> They told
> me to
> meditate

so I pretended
I was waiting
in a Doctor's
office. You
can always
pick up
a magazine
*National Geographic*
go to
China,
but I'm
here &
the breezes
admit it.
                    —"A Blue Jay," from *Not Me*

Otherwise, her work feels as if it's suffered little change; the plays and stories are a broadening of the essential form, which is the self performing and meditating on the performance. This is a saintly process, in that it's very stripped and undistracted. The protagonist does not lead a saintly life except in being poor (she doesn't want to be poor), and tends to contract towards herself rather than expand outwards into others or god, but her concentration is nonetheless of a saintly order. She identifies with the warlike St. Joan, the most active and suspect of saints:

A white dove
came out of her mouth as she died.
Five hundred and forty-eight years ago today.
A dove leaped right out of her mouth.
                    —"Joan," from *Maxfield Parrish*

Note how simple and vivid those lines are and, no, Myles didn't make it up, she read it in a book, that "a man saw white doves / fly from her mouth." Why are some poets' poems so much more alive than other poets' poems? Because the poet/person her/himself is always right there in the lines forever, at the time of the writing—there was no wall between the poet's inmost self and the poem. And Myles's mission, as I've said, continuously has been to unite her work and herself.

A "typical" Eileen Myles poem—is that fair?—a longer one,

might be "To the Maiden of Choice," from her book *Maxfield Parrish*. The title of the poem is perfectly clear and strange—what is a "maiden of choice"? *Read me and find out.* The poem announces right away that it is about whether or not one chooses one's life's conditions:

> A man
> walks in and he chose
> to die, chose to be
> a homosexual and a man,
> chose the parents
> who seeded him so,
> chose to be born
> now, in a plague.
>
> This is where the New Age
> grows fascist:
> I see, therefore
> I am.

The poem is instantly and sociologically about a "now," referring as it does to AIDS and the New Age—one finds out later that the poet is in New Mexico: has someone said or written something provoking the outburst? Probably. The transition from AIDS to the New Age is quite abrupt, though "in life" the two clang together as naturally as everything so unnatural does now. The stanza continues:

> A harmonic
> convergence of those
> who choose, the unvisioning
> leading greasy corporal lives
> prey to disease, doubt
> and age. In my
> straw hat and my
> Indian shawl I feed
> sweets to the hummingbirds
> from my blue house.
> I drive a quaint
> turquoise car and
> heal myself, so
> don't get in my way.

This is very good writing, quick and pretty and devastating, but especially quick. Almost as fast as the mind, as close to it as one can get in poetry, yet syntactically clear and fluid and both visual and talky.

The poet next posits, in a rather odd stanza (Myles's poems go all over the place, maintaining a semblance of sameness throughout), a possible life or "universe" of sixty-eight years, a life which is also a Trojan or Cretan boat sailed by a woman, a "hopeless / little boat." The poet then, in successive stanzas, contemplates one's luck at avoiding accidental deaths; the fact that great paintings seem painted by no one—she asks if they choose to be painted, for the subject of the poem is becoming "choice"; the poet's choice to eat an "old peach," presumably while writing. Now the shape of the poem, as so far established, changes, even, one might say, gets violated (this sort of violation *is* typical), when the next stanza turns out to be over two pages long. The poet is now ready to make her statement about choice and will not be hindered by an established pattern of shorter stanzas or statements, this is *the* statement, the place where the poem gives. She chose to be an alcoholic, she chose not to be one later; did she choose her own parents; how do events in her life, people met, the fact that she's in New Mexico right now, fit into this idea? In the last, also long stanza, she decides that she did choose her parents, but this is not a capricious "thing to say," born out of a New Age train of thought (New Age notions keep nudging at the poem: past lives, astrology, astral planes). It's a way of expressing an intuition of life's grandness, sacredness, mystery:

> Do I
> think I picked
> my parents. Yes.
> Because as I stood
> on my good-looking
> legs watching
> the moon
> slide in and out of
> the earth's shadow
> I teetered on the
> edge of awe and
> artifice and

during the first
scene of Callisto
I was transformed.
My parents were
sad and funny
and strong.
But I did not
choose for Massachusetts
to have pines
and Plymouth Rock.

In a way she only means she shares with her parents a love of opera, which affinity was established earlier. Myles has been to the Santa Fe Opera and seen, presumably, *Callisto;* there has also been a lunar eclipse this night. The passage repeats that practical information, but the passage is double, as it rises above its earthy geography into the heavens and a moment when time swirls rather than proceeds. The poem can now wind down, a process which doesn't take much longer. The last lines are:

And I don't believe
in God. On and
on it's a bigger
and bigger
womb. It's time
to know some
women and
come home.

In "A Maiden of Choice" as in much good poetry, one both knows and doesn't know what's being said; or sometimes (in some readings) one knows and sometimes one doesn't: the poem's transparent but oddly opaque. Whether or not the reader understands it this time, she or he, I believe, will be caught up, because the movement in the poem is compelling. An evening, a vacation, and a life are made to dance together until the life stars or triumphs, until a night at the opera and a few days in New Mexico become properly subordinate to the life's vaster scheme. This is a performance—a live act: will Myles bring the poem off, will the poem—which seems to be synonymous with the life—win again? She obviously thinks it's won since it's in the book, but will the reader think so? The reader may be used to being told by the form itself that the poem's won, at least in the case of more traditional forms. In the case of a poem like this, the reader might have to ask, is the poet right? Is the poem true? Why do I care, if I do? Why should I care about "her" and not "sestina" or "open-field" or "language"? Well the act is dangerous, for one thing. And for another the act attracts truth by being on the line, naked. Myles isn't posturing: to posture you have to sound like someone else, a known role. Unless one says that the role of poet is a posture, but that would be stupid, like saying that it's affected for you to use feet for walking. To move by natural means.

> Or I thought the ideal was the idea of astral
> projection compared to the physical
> sensation of
> flying in my dreams. I'm never
> tempted to jot down a line
> and the feeling of erupting
> poem
> in my solar plexus is simply that
> a poem coming
> & of course I'm too busy to
> fly.
> —"Ptolemy," from *Maxfield Parrish*

In the essay "How I Wrote Certain of My Poems" Myles describes writing a poem called "Hot Night":

The process of the poem, the performance of it I mentioned, is central to an impression I have that life is a rehearsal for the poem, or the final moment of spiritual revelation. I literally stepped out of my house that night, feeling a poem coming on. Incidentally, it hadn't started raining yet, so I wasn't alone in being ready to burst. I was universally pent up. I had done my research, pretty unconsciously, celebrating the mood I was in. Taking the ferry, watching the Angels, then the explosion of rain and light made it absolutely necessary to go in the deli on 6th street and buy a notebook and pen. I went over to the Yaffa and wrote it looking out the window. I haven't changed a thing. . . .

I've had this feeling before—of going out to get a poem,

like hunting. . . . As I walked I was recording the details. I was the details. I was the poem.

There are three performances to be dealt with, amalgamated: that of the life, that of writing of the poem, and finally that of performing the poem after it's written. The performance of the life, in main outline, partly entails facing up to sorrow, the consequences of bad decisions, bad trends, all the disruption, poverty, and fumbling to which anyone might be prey; the localized performance of the life, say going to the opera in New Mexico, is a conduit for the main trend and provides the particulars of the discussion. The writing of the poem itself, one guesses, is ecstatic. Ecstasy is a rather technical word here, referring to how the poet does her job. Ecstasy is what one gets, in measured doses, after giving up a great deal to be a poet. The performance of the poem after it's written is a third interesting matter to which Myles has devoted attention. Always a skilled reader of her work (in the early days in a variously good-girl candid, torchy, street-corner tough manner), she began experimenting with "performance art" in the eighties. There was an interesting period when she memorized her poems for readings, even writing long poems by a method suitable to progressive memorization, in variable mostly two- and three-line chunks:

> Everywhere I go
> is home
>
> when I'm dreaming.
> Creamy traffic
>
> pouring past
> the Noho Star
>
> *I thought you were
> coming to my
> home!*
>
> I am.
> Okay.
> —"A Poem In Two Homes," from *Not Me*

Another genre she's used is the play, beginning in the seventies with communal or collaborative theatrical projects, skit-like,

like *Patriarchy* and *Joan of Arc,* both performed at the St. Mark's Poetry Project. In the eighties she began to write various kinds of "plays" by herself, which were performed by herself with others, or by herself, in East Village venues. Finally, in 1992, she ran for president of the United States as a write-in candidate, an event presaged a few years earlier by a poem called "An American Poem," from *Maxfield Parrish,* in which she asserts that she is a secret Kennedy and "your president":

> I am a Kennedy.
> And I await
> your orders.
> You are the New Americans.
> The homeless are wandering
> the streets of our nation's
> greatest city. Homeless
> men with AIDS are among
> them. Is that right?
> That there are no homes
> for the homeless, that
> there is no free medical
> help for these men. And *women.*

The 1992 campaign involved making speeches, preparing a platform, traveling, a newsletter, the observation of the proper legal forms for a write-in candidate, the dedicating of herself in a dead-serious way to the given political process while remaining frankly in her own life and poetry.

Myles's practice may be seen as a continuous striving for unity, of moment to life to short line to poem to performance of poem already written. By stressing this bent of her work, I'm leaving a lot out, that she is a feminist and a lesbian, that that's a large part of the content of her poetry. It's disgusting that one's content must be directed by the cruelty of others. But if one's purpose is a poet's traditional one of the mediation between the soul, the serene impartial center of one, and the world with its manifold tyrannies, one will include as content the stories of a harassed and rebellious life. What else is there to talk about? On the other hand performance is everything, so form is, the line and stanza in action, a body-life moving about in front of every body, to see what happens during and after this. I've always been interested in what happens after a poem. I myself know there's no *final* moment of spiritual revelation, to end with another quibble. I'm not sure there's a final moment, so what does one take from poem to poem? Can one live in between poems? Is any one poem all of it? Is it good enough? Could I rest in just one and not leave? Perhaps Eileen Myles is trying to create the coincidence of all her poems into one, one time. Then final means only and it works.

# A Certain Slant of Sunlight

Ted Berrigan's book *A Certain Slant of Sunlight,* written during
1982 and completed six months before his death in July of 1983,
is a sequence of poems originally composed on blank postcards,
each four and a half by seven inches. As I've written in the book's
introductory note, Ken and Anne Mikolowski of the Alternative
Press had an ongoing project of sending a set of five hundred
such postcards to select people in the hopes of having the cards
returned to them with the "picture" side filled with holograph
poems and other materials. Individual cards were then included
in packets of printed broadsides, bumper stickers, and so on,
sent to the Mikolowskis' "subscribers" (the packets were free).
The point is that the cards as a constant size and shape became
for Berrigan a form, and the poems written in this form became
a sequence. The form provided for a poem that could be only as
long as the card's size permitted: if the handwriting was kept very
small you could wind up with a poem as long as *"What a Dump,*
or, Easter" (thirty-one lines, including stanza breaks); however,
most of the poems are shorter than that, in the eight- to twenty-
line range, say. A few are very much shorter, are only a line or
two lines in length, and sometimes suggestive of a postcard "message" (e.g., "SALUTATION / 'Listen, you cheap little liar'"). Is such
a form a form? There isn't much of the grid in it, to compare it
with Berrigan's *The Sonnets,* which is composed very much to a
grid. The form isn't a plan for the deployment of words and lines
so much as an approach, an ambience, maybe a tone. Yet there
are qualities in the poems' general method which suggest *The
Sonnets* and which suggest a fidelity to the sense of the self presented in *The Sonnets.* But *A Certain Slant of Sunlight* isn't about

---

Review of Ted Berrigan's *A Certain Slant of Sunlight* (Oakland: O Books,
1988). From *American Poetry Review* 28 (March–April 1999).

"art" as *The Sonnets* often seems to be, it's about dying and about community; it's about wreckage and salvage, and about states of consciousness that shouldn't be dealt with according to rules.

The poems in *A Certain Slant of Sunlight* tend to be composed of units of information, or stories which stand for something else, or bits of language suggestive of emotional states, happenstance, philosophy, reflectiveness. They are haunted by other people's lines, lines by dead greats and lines by Berrigan's friends (who were often invited to write a few words on the cards). *The Sonnets* is characterized by the use of lines as units of information and knowledge and by the use of other people's lines, but also by the constant repetition of such lines; there is no such repetition in *A Certain Slant of Sunlight*. Repetition, classically, destroys linear time and establishes a simulacrum of the flow of consciousness. *A Certain Slant* works by creating singular structures; as a sequence it is held together by what might be called its knowingness (the author of *The Sonnets* didn't know very much, in a way—he was only in his late twenties—and the book's knowledge flows from its strict formalism as if tapped from an unconscious which isn't quite the author's). Doug Oliver once suggested to me that a typical Berrigan poem is a cognition, that is, a piece of knowledge or consciousness, a sort of "clicking in." *The Sonnets* are loose seen in this way; the poems in *A Certain Slant* are tight:

### Poets Tribute to Philip Guston

> I hear walking in my legs
> Aborigines in the pipes
> I am the man your father was
> Innocence bleats at my last
> Black breaths—and tho I was considered a royal
> pain in the ass by
> Shakespeare's father, the high alderman,
> All the deadly virtuous plague my death!
> I could care less?

This is not pretty, sublime, or classical (though some of the others of the poems could be so described); it's both mysterious and blatant, and by virtue of the poet's proximate death extremely serious.

I've often wondered why people don't seem to notice this book so much, as it is one of Berrigan's three major sequences. (*Easter Monday* has never been published as the sequence Berrigan intended; almost all of its comprising poems have been published separately.) *The Sonnets* is esthetically perfect, being based on an idea, and there has been increasingly a taste for such work recently. Berrigan considered *The Sonnets* to be somewhat self-educational, and it is, but that isn't necessarily a drawback. *The Sonnets*, though, is a book that hasn't been properly understood or at least described, and in that lack of understanding may be found the reasons why *A Certain Slant* is neglected. *The Sonnets* is not, as is sometimes stated, concerned with the rejection of the "psychological I"; the psychological I is right there in the book in all its life-plots and circumstances and all its emotional field but stretched across time, warped in time, twisting and doubling back and pushing on into the future rather like karma. In all of Berrigan's work thereafter, and certainly in *A Certain Slant*, the I of it can be large and contemplative or more ordinarily small or, actually usually, both at once. In Berrigan there is a metaphysical I—the transcendent watcher; a presentational I—the character of the ordinary man who buys the *Post* at Gem's Spa to read the sports page; and an I which is deeply entangled in the stories it participates in with others. At death one might be particularly concerned with the latter, since one's responsibilities to others and theirs to one traditionally loom large then. In *A Certain Slant* a "caught" person is speaking, someone caught in the traps of the psychological I (and really, who isn't?), someone enraged and loving who is about to have to leave.

*A Certain Slant* is an "unpleasant" book, in the Shavian sense. It covers a year in the life of a poet who is soon to die in poverty though close in the arms of family, but in the midst of unpleasant arguments with fellow members of an artistic community, in an increasingly venal decade. It isn't generally recognized that he is dying, and he speaks of it only slantwise, as in these poems. He is "on drugs"; he is, as the above poem suggests, past caring what others think but not about the proper way to do his job, the poet's job. This "plot" or line throughout the poems is not explicit but is ever pointed at; it isn't ennobled or aggrandized. The author isn't showing off with language for example, things are too extreme for that, though not for having fun with words sometimes. The title "Poets Tribute to Philip Guston" refers to an event during the previous year, a tribute to the recently dead abstract expressionist painter which was held at the St. Mark's Poetry Project. Many people participated; all were counseled to limit their performances to five minutes. Berrigan thought this ridiculous given Guston's philosophy of art and, especially, his art itself: a tidy package of tribute? So he rambled on and on as if a helpless speedfreak until the audience got mad at him and began booing, at which time he turned his presentation into a "statement" about excess, greatness, proportion, and how long it might take for an abstract expressionist to get to the point (remember all those stories about how long such a painter might agonize before and during painting, and really was it ever finished?). He made a mess and he cleaned it up, deliberately. There are people who attended who still don't believe he did it deliberately; his performance that evening is still a scandal; the transcript of the evening which he hired someone to type from the tape is still unpublished. Can this rather small poem mean all of that? The first two lines suggest a Guston, heaps of tubes and shoes, a can-these-bones-live type of thing, and also a creaky person (Berrigan had a bad back and a bad ankle); I am the man your father was, that is, Guston (a lot of the you's in the book are fellow poets, younger than Berrigan even if of the same poetry "generation," "youngsters" who are down on him). "Innocence bleats at my last / Black" and then whoever Shakespeare's father is (what tightass is that?) is really being put down, possibly by Shakespeare himself . . . all the deadly virtuous, *yes my friends you, and I am dying, and I don't have time for your censure.* There is a lot of weight on the "innocence bleats" line and on the "deadly virtuous" line: the first is full of self-justification and self-torture, the second is quite killing. Yet the poem is also small, and light. Poetry isn't supposed to be like that right now; it's supposed to be monumental. Not epigrammatic, that can't be great—not cutting as if cutting to a real person in a real situation.

The poems are in a fairly chronological order, so part of one's reading of the book is as a progress through the seasons and a literal year. There are also themes: the censuring of clerk and bookkeeper types of poets; the arrivals of visitors; the proximity of beloveds and friends who no longer seem to be those; the Poetry Project (a layered phrase); the deaths of others; politics outside the community; the past. There's a lot of love in the book but also a constant accusatory element, as if the community at hand is not being loving enough, mirroring too the contemporary world. The untitled second poem in the book has a history of unpleasantness behind it though not in it:

> You'll do good if you play it like you're
> >not getting paid.
> But you'll do it better if the motherfuckers pay you.
>
> (Motto of THE WHORES
> & POETS GUILD—trans.
> from The Palatine Anthology by Alice Notley &
> Ted Berrigan. 20 Feb 82)

It was censored out of *The World,* the magazine of the Poetry Project, in 1982, which fact is one of the main reasons it appears second in the book, that and because it is a motto and an unromantic statement that poets are rarely paid for their "services." In contrast, the fourth poem in the book is the widely anthologized title poem, a classic and deeply felt "good poem" which is about the illness and imminent death of the poet's mother, though that is never mentioned except indirectly:

> . . . the tall pretty girl in the print dress
> under the fur collar of her cloth coat will be standing
> by the wire fence where the wild flowers grow not too tall
> her eyes will be deep brown and her hair styled 1941 American
> >will be too; but
> I'll be shattered by then

The allusion is to a photograph, but it is called "the picture": what does it mean that "mother and son, 33 & 7, First Communion Day, 1941" will be, literally, "on St. Mark's Place" (where the poet resided) when the poet goes there "tomorrow," though "I'll go out for a drink with one of my demons tonight . . . in Colorado 1980 spring snow"? This poem, like some others in the book, was written earlier than 1982 but in a sense was written again when inscribed on a postcard (its form changed by its becoming a "postcard poem"). Berrigan's mother's lung cancer commenced in 1980, and she was expected to die that year but lasted until July 1982, a year to the month before his own death. The poem states that he will meet himself and his past, meeting her death on St. Mark's Place (he expected to be there when she died), but there is also an eerie suggestion of his own death and of her and his meeting in death in an everlasting First Communion.

I'm tempted to proceed through the book poem by poem discussing each one because they are so different from each other, but there's obviously not space for that here. "The Einstein Intersection," another poem towards the beginning, "looks" a little like the title poem but isn't in the least like it:

This distinguished boat
Now for oblivion, at sea, a
Sweet & horrid joke in dubious taste,
That once, a Super-Ego of strength, did both haunt
Your dreams and also save you much bother, brought
You to the American Shore; Out of The Dead City carried you,
Free, Awake, in Fever and in Sleep, to the
City of A Thousand Suns where, there, in the innocent heart's
Cry & the Mechanized Roar of one's very own this, The 20th
      Century, one's
Own betrayed momentary, fragmented Beauty got
Forgotten, one Snowy Evening, Near a Woods, because
The Horse Knows the Way; because of, "The Hat on the Bed," and
Because of having "Entered the Labyrinth, finding No Exit.", is
That self-same ship, the "U.S.S. Nature" by name, that D. H. Lawrence
      wrote one of his very best poems about;
THE SHIP OF DEATH; (a/k/a THE CAT CAME BACK)!

The distinguished boat which becomes the ship of death is a compound of body, soul, and ambition and personality, as striven for and then lost; desire and struggle lead to loss, revealing the collapse of the body and the true identity of the self as the ship of death, an ambiguity of course. The poem is labyrinthine like life, justifying the reference to a sonnet of Petrarch's that Berrigan once translated with George Schneeman: "Entered the Labyrinth, finding No Exit." After the deathy opening lines one meets with a succession of literary references generating each other through associational processes. I'm not sure of all the references; the title, "The Einstein Intersection," and "Out of The Dead City" and "City of A Thousand Suns" refer to works by Samuel R. Delany, the science fiction writer and a friend, but there are references also to Frost's poem "Stopping by Woods on a Snowy Evening," to the children's song which begins "Over the river and through the woods to grandmother's house we go," to the Petrarch sonnet, to the Lawrence poem, and to a popular song ("the cat came back"). Lawrence's poem's ending hints of rebirth, the cat coming back? Or is the cat coming back death after all? The language of this poem is strangely thrilling though the tone is ironic; it's composed of the odds and ends of thinking, the connections the head often makes when not trying to think about something. Berrigan always asserted that he thought in words and that when he wasn't thinking in words he was reading. I don't particularly believe this assertion refers to what goes on in the mind, I think it refers to a sort of self-training, on his part, in being conscious either of words or of nothing, because thinking is useless, blocks action, stirs up messy unhelpful emotion, etc.—or so he thought. "The Einstein Intersection" impels the reader through long lines clotted with capitalized phrases which stop one for split-seconds of recognition, cognition: will the reader make it? and does of course, along and hovering and towards feeling slightly gotten at in such lines as "the Mechanized Roar of one's very own this, The 20th Century." Yes, we've all held it close.

A poem like "Joy of Shipwrecks," which appears further along in the book in what one might think of as the early spring section, is, like "The Einstein Intersection," starred with phrases and words where layered events, small concatenations of meanings, light up, but these are subtler and certainly not capitalized:

Stoop where I sit, am crazy
in sunlight on, brown as stone,
like me, (stoned, not brown; I
am white, like writer trash), see
that stick figure, chalky, also
white, with tentative grin, walking
toward us? Feel your blood stirring?

That's Eileen, as typical as sunlight
in the morning; typical as the morning
the morning after a typical Eileen night

If the reader remembers "The Einstein Intersection" when approaching "Joy of Shipwrecks" it will be wondered if it is the
Ship of Death that has been wrecked and if so whether that
means death or life. The first phrase is really funny—"Stoop
where I sit"—since a stoop is a place, a posture, and a lowering
of one's standards; the "I" of the poem—is it the poet or the
dedicatee?—is "crazy / in sunlight" but is that good or bad? "I /
am white, like writer trash" alludes to both "poor white trash"
and crumpled paper in a writer's wastepaper basket. The word
"white" keeps changing as a "stick figure, chalky, also / white"
approaches the stoop: "white" is a race now but is also beginning to mean something like "hungover" or white after a long
debauched night. The stick figure becomes "Eileen" and the
word "Eileen" becomes "I lean," because of "Stoop where I sit"
(and because Berrigan always thought of the name that way).
But "Eileen" is as "typical as sunlight / in the morning," "Eileen"
is made to seem positive; everything feels crazy and wrecked,
poor and wrecked, as well as joyous and wrecked. Berrigan was
leaning a lot the last few years of his life; he was running out of
time and so was trying to get everything said and taken care of.
This involved a lot of leaning on others, leaning in on, pressur-
ing of people to listen, people who didn't know he was dying
since he wasn't doing it in the conventional way, that is, with a
final diagnosis, a doctor, a hospital. This poem doesn't quite say
that, but taken with the other poems it does.

I've been showing how certain poems work and what their
background is. These have so far been "poem" poems, by which
I mean almost traditional poems in that they look and sound
like poems and are written in complete (sometimes obsessively
complete and byzantinely claused) sentences. There are also
"idea" poems, such as "People Who Change Their Names,"
which is essentially a list of names with punctuation. Another
idea poem is "Tough Cookies," which is a list of simple sentences that might be inserted in fortune cookies, inspired by
Frank O'Hara's poem "Lines for the Fortune Cookies," and containing such lines as

You have strange friends, but
they are going to be strangers.

Everything is Maya, but
you will never know it.

Your gaiety is not cowardice,
but it may be hepatitis.

Berrigan, incidentally, died of cirrhosis of the liver, a condition which usually is, and had been, preceded by a ghastly session of hepatitis. On the next page after "Tough Cookies," in what is probably the autumn part of the book, is a poem called "Skeats and the Industrial Revolution," written in the peculiar non-syntax of the dictionary definition. The title of course is a play on "Keats and the Industrial Revolution"; beneath the title are the words "(DICK JEROME, 3/4 View) / ink on paper," since the artist Dick Jerome had provided an image for the postcard on which the work was written. The definition from Skeats's *Etymological Dictionary* which the poem takes off from is of "god":

> *God:* perhaps, 'The being worshipped. To
> whom sacrifice is offered. Not allied to
> 'good,' (which is an adjective, not a
> 'being.' *Godwit:* a bird, or, more recently,
> a 'twittering-machine'; (from the Anglo-Saxon,
> *God-wiht:* just possibly meaning, 'worthy creature.'
> Viz. Isle of Wight—Isle of Creatures. See, also,
> *Song, folk;* Childe Ballad #478: "I've been
> a creature for a thousand years.". . . .)

This is a dense, allusive gathering of language about deity, worship, song (poetry), and nature, in a light enough tone, but Berrigan is always also serious and these are serious words being defined. Not all of the words come from Skeats, of course. "Twittering-machine," for example, is a phrase used by Peter Schjeldahl in a book review (it's really a Paul Klee title) to describe certain of my own poems from the seventies. The word "creature" also has a history of reference to myself: I have an early poem called "Creatures" and often preferred the word, in playful conversation, to words like "people" or "humans." There is in *A Certain Slant,* earlier on, a poem called "Creature," dedicated to me, which is a parodic rewriting of one of my better-known poems,

"When I Was Alive." The last reference in the work, "I've been / a creature for a thousand years," is a rewrite of a line by the singer/musician/composer Neil Young: "I've been a miner for a thousand years." (The singer is "searching for a heart of gold," gold being another word sounding like god or good or godwit though it's omitted. "Childe" probably suggested "Young," another word not quite included.) The poem implies that there is a god, that god is not the same as good since god is more than a human adjective, and that a bird or poet is possessed by god or godwit, though also a mere creature whose life seems endless.

Among the poems which might be called stories, descriptions which stand for something else, is "In Morton's Grille," a reminiscence of a cafe in which a machine might play a three-minute movie of a purported episode from the feud between the Hatfields and McCoys:

> & a zany 3 minute movie of the Hatfields
> shooting at the McCoys out a log cabin
> window came on; the McCoys ran out of
> bullets, so they started singing, "Pass the
> Biscuits, Mirandy!" Grandma's biscuits were
> so hard, terrible, but saved the day when thrown
> at the real McCoys.

Those are the last seven lines of the thirteen-line poem; it isn't hard to guess that the poem is meant to be about feuds; as I've indicated before, Berrigan was involved at the time in a handful of, how can one put it, not feuds all of them, but situations involving bad feeling stemming from seemingly small incidents. The poems that deal with them are clean and inscrutable:

### Montezuma's Revenge

> In order to make friends with the natives
> In my home town, I let them cut off my face
> By the shores of Lake Butter, on
> The 7th anniversary of their arrival
> In our Utopia. It was the First of May.
> Nose-less, eye-less, speechless, and
> With no ears, I understood their reasoning.
> And will spend the rest of my days
> helping them cover their asses. Free.

In this poem the speaker has been longer in his Utopia than "the natives," a reminder that invaders of new lands often quickly become not only the governors of them but the new definition of what a native or citizen is. Any community can be taken over and redefined; old-timers are often asked not to be who they are, not to represent anything threatening, not to have force or claim intelligence. In another poem, called "In Your Fucking Utopias," the very idea of a utopia seems to represent exclusion:

> Let the heart of the young
>     exile the heart of the old: Let the heart of the old
> Stand exiled from the heart of the young: Let
>     other people die: Let Death be inaugurated.
> Let there be Plenty Money. & Let the
> Darktown Strutters pay their way in
> To the Gandy-Dancers Ball. But Woe unto you, O
>     Ye Lawyers, because I'll be there, and
>             I'll be there.

The opening lines are from Whitman's poem "Respondez!" and a Whitmanic/Ginsbergian voice is used in several of the poems, as if the sound itself were a kind of subject, a comment on generosity and where Berrigan had come to find it lacking. Such poems are played off against the book's several overtly political poems, one being "Mutiny!" about the Falkland Islands War, containing lines by the British poet Tom Pickard:

> they kept rolling over, be-
> neath the tracer bullets and
> the Antarctic moon, beneath the
> daunting missiles and the Prince
> in his helicopter, they were
> steaming toward interesting places,
> to meet interesting people, and
> kill them. They were at sea,
> and it was also beneath them.

"They" sound chillingly like the new arrivals at the shores of Lake Butter. Colonization in the poetry world takes place frequently, though it's always a small event in the eyes of others, who by treating such events as small would make poetry small. The Falkland Islands War, too, was very small; it was, certainly, beneath the attention of most people. One poem that Berrigan loved to read was "To Sing the Song, That Is Fantastic," a reggae influenced by the singer Yellowman, about Caribbeans selling M-16s to French Canadians:

> The soldiers shoot the old woman
>> down
> They shoot the girl-child on
>> the ground: we
> Steal & sell the M-16s, use
> The money to buy the weed
> The sky is blue & the Erie is
>> Clean;
> Come to us with your M-16

It's possible that the book's very short poems create an illusion that the book is slight. The short poem was a form dear to Berrigan's intellect; his influences in this field were initially Kerouac and Ungaretti. He came to see the form as a vehicle for meditation and perfection since every part, every piece of every letter of every word, is apparent. But the haiku has felt banalized lately, the short poem seems often directed towards jokes, and again it is a time that seems to prefer either large-scale, personally ambitious poems whose concerns are very general or that descriptive poem that's really prose which continues to haunt the mainstream:

*Windshield*

There is no windshield.

This is funny and bleak; the word "windshield" becomes perfectly opaque and then ridiculous: what on earth could a "windshield" be? One pictures a knight holding it up, though the original drawing by George Schneeman (reproduced on the cover of the book) suggests something as fragile as the fan of a Japanese court lady. The poem is obviously in key with the deathiness of the whole book, but it's also perfectly light.

*Okay. First. . . .*

"Truth is that which,
Being so, does do its
work."
(I said That.)

The first thing, the fundamental thing, is truth, a working active beingness; it's much better said in the poem, much clearer, isn't it? "I said That." The capital *T* changes the emphasis: the said truth became different from its speaker, because it was the truth. Those two positions may be contradictory; on the other hand, there they are in the same poem.

*Jo-Mama*

The St. Mark's Poetry Project
is closed for the summer. But
all over the world, poets
are writing poems. Why?

This is a poem directed against the provincialism of poetry communities even in a city like New York. Two important words are "world" and "Why." One rather faint voice in the poem is saying, why bother to write poems if our all-important poetry center is closed; the dominant answering voice states that poetry is an immense community, worldwide and ancient, in which one's own group is a tiny speck.

I have been leaving out all of the "nice" poems, warm with friendship feelings, fatherly feelings, and love. There are poems which celebrate visits by Joanne Kyger and by English poet friends (Pickard, and Wendy Mulford, Denise Riley, and Doug Oliver, in New York for a poetry festival); there are poems with and for the children and myself; there are two lovely poems with/about Allen Ginsberg and Peter Orlovsky; there are funny Christmas messages to Barrett Watten and Carla Harryman, and to Jim and Rosemary Carroll. There is an almost literally warm poem for Anne Waldman and Reed Bye, called "Dinosaur Love":

Anne Lesley Waldman says, No Fossil Fuels
The best of the free times are still yet to come

> With all of our running & all of our coming if we
> Couldn't laugh we'd both go insane—with changes
>     of attitudes
> At the Horse Latitudes—if we couldn't laugh, we'd
>     All be insane —
> but right here with you, the living seems true, &
> the gods are not burning us just to keep warm.

I'd like to conclude by invoking the beginning and ending of the book, both of which are quasi-religious and complicated. The book was meant to contain, in fact, at its beginning, a copy of a horoscope cast for Ted in 1981; I believe it was omitted because it didn't reproduce very well. It would have been a sort of graphic signifying fatedness, a map or plan for temperament born in the stars: that itself signifying all manner of things that can't be helped, among which I think Berrigan might have included class, talent (even genius), certain deep-seated character traits. As a result of which, the reader might have concluded, it has come to this, this final book. The very first poem, called "Poem," is:

> Yea, though I walk
> through the Valley of
> the Shadow of Death, I
> Shall fear no evil —
> for I am a lot more
> insane than
> This Valley.

The poem, a rather tonally blasphemic invocation of the Twenty-third Psalm, suggests Whitman's characterization of death, in "When Lilacs Last in the Dooryard Bloom'd," as "sane and sacred." The poem does sound slightly insane, at least shaky; Berrigan believed in being overt since that was truthful, and one of his favorite lines of poetry was Roethke's "This shaking keeps me steady." (Berrigan's hands trembled when he read his poems in public.) The last two poems in the book are December poems, Christmas poems. Here is the second-to-last, called "Christmas Card (for Barry & Carla)":

Take me, third factory of life!
But don't put me in the wrong guild.
So far my heart has borne even
the things I haven't described.

Never be born, never be died.

The "right guild," if you'll remember from the beginning, from the previously censored second poem, is the "Whores & Poets Guild": Berrigan never wanted to belong to a different one. "Never be born, never be died," a phrase of Buddhist sentiment (and Berrigan had both a strong Buddhist and a strong Christian streak), was remembered by Berrigan for years from a tiny pamphlet by a Japanese artist/poet whose name I don't know. The final poem, called "Poem," gives the book to the general world, its meaning to the body politic:

The Nature of the Commonwealth
the whole body of the People
flexed her toes and
breathed in pine.

I'm the one that's so
radical, 'cause all I do is pine. Oh I just
can't think of anything–
No politics. No music. Nobody. Nothing but sweet

Romance. Per se. De gustibus non disputandum est.
Flutters eyelashes. Francis, my house is falling down.
Repair it. Merry Christmas.

The Whores & Poets Guild is similar to the Franciscan order in that it vows poverty and a certain kind of obedience (to principle, you might say), it is itinerant and begging, its members can seem crazy, indeed what seems to be insane might turn out to be exemplar, as some of the stories in *The Little Flowers of St. Francis*. The "Whores" part simply has to do with money, the poet's practice of prostitution (who doesn't?)—Berrigan was never a courtesan, he was a whore. The "Whores" part also has to do with the body and one's "use" of it simply to keep going, via speed for example, often for the sake of others. The body, like a whore's body, then breaks down relatively early. Whores and other reprobates and scum were of course the core of early Christianity; they, and soldiers, for example, are the *used* people, used and cast off. This poem is flirty and sexy too, like a whore? The Nature of the Commonwealth is calling on Francis, at any rate, to repair Her house. Thus the book ends not with the call of death (which was coming soon) but with the call to the poet's task again.

*A Certain Slant of Sunlight* is an important book because, for one thing, it's the only one like it. It faces death and observes the community through a various kind of poem which is true to the life being led. Also, it's the repository of a number of personal virtues one might care to emulate or be inspired by. And may I ask where such virtues, manifestly existing, fit into a philosophy which disallows the psychological I? The psychological I is that which by making terrible mistakes learns how to live and be generous, out of its very self, its I. But back to the specific virtues of this book. It complains but it isn't selfish or even self-centered; it's thoroughly alive; it's prophetic, low-life, and entertaining. It's very deep if you know how to find depth in poetry; it's courageous, and since it's that, the reader can take courage from it too. Furthermore, the language, the form (they seem to be simultaneous) of the poems is extraordinary in its ability to negotiate quick dense changes and still maintain transparency and the brevity necessitated by the postcards. These poems suggest a direction in poetry that has yet to be picked up: we've all been too obsessed with being "important." But importance isn't necessarily where you think it is; it's really generated by circumstance and is in the flesh and spirit of the poems, not in a presentation of "importance." *These* are important poems.

I'd like to point out that in the poem "Interstices," which is a flashback to the method of *The Sonnets,* Berrigan says "call me Berrigan." I've obeyed the request: it's created enough distance for me to see the full worth of the work.

# Iovis Omnia Plena

With the publication of Book II of *Iovis* last spring, Anne Waldman's poem is now 648 pages long. Book I contains twenty-
three and Book II contains twenty-five individual poems or sections of varying lengths, as short as three or four pages, as long
as twenty. Each section is preceded by an italicized head, a
third-person plot summary also containing parallel information, side facts. The prevailing form for a section is an amalgam
of verse and prose, the latter including letters from others, selections from interviews, dream narratives, journalistic fact, and
so forth, though some of the sections are in a more homoge-
neous form, repeated stanzas say, or a consistently surfaced
"score" for a performance. It is difficult in fact not to project
into the silent reading of the work, at almost any point, the
sound of a Waldman performance: the whole work is a score, as
well as a poem for the silent reader, with no loss of quality and
force in either aspect. The theme of the poem is male energy
and power, the fact of its dominion over all of us in both the
harmful and so-called harmless forms, and most specifically the
author's relation to it in her personal and professional life. In a
way the form of the poem is Waldman's ongoing life, as in
Frank O'Hara's sentence "What is happening to me . . . goes
into my poems." However, what is happening to Waldman is experienced by her as mythic as well as quotidian, and she identifies with many more personages, real and imaginary, than herself in the course of this investigation, passing among an array
of cultures and vantages.

  Is the poem rightfully to be called an epic? That probably

Review of Anne Waldman's *Iovis*, Book I (Minneapolis: Coffee House
Press, 1993) and *Iovis*, Book II (Minneapolis: Coffee House Press,
1997). From *Chicago Review* 44, no. 1 (1998).

depends on how picky you are about your definition. In "Both, Both: An Introduction," at the beginning of Book I, Waldman acknowledges "a debt & challenge of epic masters Williams, Pound, Zukovsky, Olson," as well as a more indirect debt to H. D.'s *Helen in Egypt*. I myself wonder if the first four of those authors have written what can rightfully be called epics since their works contain, really, no story and have rather than a continuity of narrative and form a continuity of consciousness. There is a letter towards the beginning of Book II of *Iovis* which brings up the question of definition in a different way. The writer of the letter, K, has participated in a class taught by Robert Creeley, one of Waldman's specific heroes in *Iovis* and also certainly a friend, in which he seems to have eliminated *Iovis* from the category of epic on the basis of the poet's "ego": Waldman does not manage to transcend hers, Olson in *The Maximus Poems* does. K writes that "what he meant is that your work is more personal in that you bring in letters, stories about your child, emotional instances, etc." As the letter makes clear, a male definition of ego/egolessness tends to be a little special. My sense is that Waldman's form is close enough to that of those four masters to be called epic if you're willing to call their poems epics, and most American poetry specialists are. *Iovis* is big in spirit and scope, it includes history, it's very long, and it's replete with an appropriate grandeur of language frequently undercut, in the twentieth-century manner established by those same men, by ironies inherent in being American.

Why would a woman write a feminist poem in a male form? Why isn't this poem in one of the newer exploratory ("subversive," postmodernist, more impersonal) forms in which many women (e.g., Scalapino, Dahlen, Susan Howe, Hejinian) are now working, often writing long and even very long poems as well? The reason women are writing at such length is the need to say all the things that have been suppressed for so long, to invent mythologies themselves, to devise a world in which their imaginations actually participate. But why do so in the modernist male form? Because, if this is the form that the "greats" worked in, if this form is acknowledged as the "great" one of our (at least American) century, surely a woman can be "great" using it, as great as any man. The form, it must be acknowledged, is still wonderfully serviceable, a collaged entity which seems able to manage any juxtaposition of material, sound, and tone, and which is welcoming to most kinds of novelty of line and layout. All of that is also the form's weakness: it tempts endless heterogeneity and in its fragmentation makes little room for whatever unity there is in actual existence. I myself think there is quite a bit of unity in actual existence, and also that an epic by definition is a presentation of unity to whatever culture the epic serves. However, that's just me. I'm perfectly willing to accept Waldman as being on the grand level of my heroes Williams, Olson, etc., where she dialogues with them in radiant language. They must include her now—we must let her be included there among them, or their ranks will remain sick from lack of the female; that is, she is in the process of restoring that poetry to health.

There is a very good reason for a woman's use of her own life events to make an epic, the fact that she has nothing much else specifically female to work with, since "all is full of Jove":

> You speak my own thoughts always. The tracks
> in my own mind remind you to speak. I listen
> to you ranting, and dream myself dressing in
> front of a mirror.
> —X, "Revenge," from Book I

The details of her daily life are a woman's story when hardly anything else is, hardly anything legendary or generalizing, the readymade sense of position and importance that informs the male story. Waldman ransacks other cultures for generalizing myths about women, but her own life, being an interesting and various one, contains more possibility than the female stories she calls on, the Navajo myth of Spider Woman, or the Gaelic song of the Hag of Beare, or the not-quite-mythic notion of the trobairitz or female troubadour. At the beginning Waldman's specific purpose is to explore and celebrate where possible the ways of Jove, mainly because those seem to be the only ways to explore, but her own story comes more and more to dominate the poem, mediated through mythology and made urgent through personal crisis. Waldman's method in Book I involves the invocation and participation of her father, John, a gentle masculine figure who fought in bloody circumstance in World

War II. Through his agency, his life, war is discussed and con-
demned; thus one of the most moving events of the poem is
John's death in Book II:

> if it could be put
> how simply could it ever be put
> putting feet on ground put
> head to pillow the cold hospital
> down honorably a load for
> a body put its mark
> shadow putty
> puts its remarkable weight
> which is frail, still now
> for the marking
> no trace but what
> haunts her like a mirror
> her father's sperm
> that makes her breathe
> —IX, "Ancestor, Ancestor"

In a poem which used "history" in the academically approved
way the poet would be exploring the records of the past and
"John" would be an ordinary man discovered by accident in cen-
turies-old annals of a town, Gloucester, Massachusetts, say, and
how fascinating it would seem to speculate on his life and significance! But why can't the same significance be found in the present and in one's own life? The risks taken by the author are extraordinary: you write about your father but he dies in the
middle of your poem. You write about your relationships with
men and one crucial one is severed in the middle of your poem.
Everyone sees you; then there's thankfully nothing left to hide.
In "Both, Both: An Introduction" Waldman states, "I feel myself
always an open system (woman) available to any words or
sounds I'm informed by. A name. A date. Images of war. Other
languages to which the ear attunes." In order to be open to the
outside, the inside has to be bared. As this quote indicates,
Waldman's poem is as mediumistic as it is self-expressive. It tells
what the culture tells her to—thus the inclusion of letters, quotations, and whatever language catches her fancy, as well as the
events of her life lived in the culture. In such a work what's new

isn't going to be the author's own ideas (that's only one way to conduct a mind): it's going to be what happens next.

The structure of the individual sections can be fascinating, being never predictable: "Mom, you're so random" is one of the little motifs of Book II, something the author's son Ambrose likes to say. In section XV of Book II, "Devil's Working Overtime," that slogan is subtly recurrent, and Waldman's method of making supposedly random elements cohere is explored. Waldman and her son are in the Virgin Islands, where she is working with a group of writers and where mother and son are also swimming, snorkeling, and stargazing. The section opens with what seems to be a verbatim transcript of a local radio preacher:

> the Devil's workin overtime
> the Devil's workin overtime
> He's workin harder'n he did a year ago
> Yes, that's sure
> hmmmmmm that sure is true. . . .

Immediately juxtaposed to that passage are a short description of the snorkeling son, who claims to have seen a great barracuda (the Devil?), a fact or two about the history of the islands, a vignette of a chat on the beach with a woman who's channeling a spirit named Emmanuel. The random is spookily connected from the beginning here; the quotidian is haunted by myth. Then the first of several lists of Virgin Islands–ish things: "termite nest," "poison apples," "slave quarters," "Valiumed out," ending with the prayer "that this ode not erode." Then a passage still evocative of the setting alludes to Waldman's father's death, asserts her own resemblance to the fish that are everywhere about them, and invokes images of her own birth. In the same passage the student writers' voices enter with short dream accounts; soon there are more bits of local history, more lists and descriptions of wildlife, followed by a suddenly frontal rendering of the author and son as fishlike or amphibious:

> All of a sudden I faced "it"
> took the robe off
> & the garment was a mirror
> of myself

saw my whole self in it
and faced my whole fish self
in facing it
& We were separate
. . . . . . . . . . . . . . . .

and I watched my son
amphibian
his rubber feet—
now webbed—
emerge from sea

son of the sea of her great foam

The genesis of land creatures from the sea, and the genesis of the author from her father and her son from her, are thus performed, neatly, out of dailiness, without academic effort. The next few pages of the poem display a diagrammatical burst of names of the constellations, all over the place, "all out on the map, named & delivered to sky / because we study in reverse & code a name, color it, it seeps in / marrow-down, and then look up. . . ." The page and the sky mirror each other, as the robe and the body in the previous passage mirror each other. The sermon from the beginning of the section now starts to recur in conjunction with the idea of the stars themselves being birthed, "*o yeah they working*"; when Waldman tries to tell her son about the births of stars he counters, "Mom, you're so random," and so, fuguelike, the motifs become denser. Waldman continuously presses the poem to become itself: "work this / doesn't work it will, though / working words till they work." At the point at which the latter lines occur it's obvious that the poem has found its form, has been delivered. It ends with a prose story by Ambrose entitled "A Day in the Life of a Malaria-Carrying Mosquito," an energetic preadolescent exercise in "fiction" from the point of view of a mosquito, female, in Port Moresby who manages to eat some blood, lose a lover to Raid, and finally get swatted: any being's life story, insect, fish, mammal, perhaps even star. The section is all mirrors now, but not in a sense of parallelisms so much as in a sense of implications, connections. It isn't the estrangement of an image in the mirror that's emphasized but its relatedness; Waldman's poetry always works towards health and, in spite of its being piecemeal, wholeness. The language of Ambrose's story is not at all lofty or poetic, certainly not mature, but it belongs in a poem about mother and son: why shouldn't he speak too and have fun? When he gets the last word the poem gets the last word, rather than the poet, perhaps because innocence is allowed a proper position counter to "the devil" and innocence doesn't really speak the way, say, Blake does, like a poet.

The mirrorings and echoes and spiraling stars of "Devil's Working Overtime" reflect the structure of *Iovis* as a whole. The work never comes to a point, because it's faithful to the life process; dramatic personal events make for dramatic points in the work, but they are unanticipated, as in a life happening now, and can't be fed into a linear overview. The reader is not allowed the old pleasure of plotted development and resolution but is instead asked to recognize the recurrent forms and happenstances of phenomena. Book I ends with a sense of a change won after considerable personal stress and the dissolution of a marriage. The closing section, XXIII, "You Reduce Me to an Object of Desire," calls on the circular form of the whole poem as a means of gaining power over being an "object":

> For what got clearer was architecture, was my power &
>     that if you kept
> coming back around section by section you'd reach my
>     ultimate protest
> which reduced me to an object of desire.
>
> (Not.)
>
> You reduce me to an object of desire. But I come back
>     again. Never reject
> any thing. You reduce me to an object of desire. Never
>     reject anyone. . . .

The "you" in that passage is the "twin" or male to whom the author has now proved her equality: "villains, brothers, saints, deities." As the poem itself is built and becomes more powerful, the "you" comes back around each time, each section, to confront the author and to find her more desirable through the act of confrontation. Waldman both accepts and refutes (her professed motto is "both, both") being that object of desire, the refutation being couched in the *Wayne's World* (Ambrose's world) witticism "Not." In saying "Never reject anyone," Waldman identifies being rejected in love with being intellectually rejected and with being socially and politically rejected, since much of the book is a cry of outrage against forms of contemporary injustice. Book I ends with the sentence "To blunt the knife," as if by a circular or repeated process something might realistically be blunted, whereas in the climax of a linear story, a male story, the enemy is conquered and the weapon is seized, but that isn't real. Poetry's effects on life are gained through a gradual process, not an instantaneous one. Book II ends in a shakiness which is perhaps more truthful to life than resolution is. The last section of the book, XXV, "Sprechstimme (Countess of Dia)," proclaims itself in the italicized head to be a "sprechblues," a cross between Schoenberg's operatic spoken-sung technique and the speech-wise phrasing of such singers as Billie Holiday and Nina Simone. It has a fairly consistent musical surface, comprised of lines which sometimes hang together in the usual way, sometimes are demarcated with equals signs and made to have more space around them so that a special articulation is implied:

> =illusory shadow of love?=
>
> =did I but dream his face his cock his sound?=
>
> =it is the sounds in love?=
>
> =the words=
>
> =he did grab me with his words=
> =entered the secret place in another language=

The poet's lover has been unfaithful and she bemoans this. The section is structured inside a time zone of not-quite-simultaneous settings and circumstances. There is scrutiny of the life and work of the female troubadour, the Countess de Dia; there is a poetry conference in Vancouver, which provides certain kinds of thoughts and references and the simplest formal clue to the poem: "you understand all these words are from a notebook / three by two and one-half inches / given to me by Ann Lauterbach"; there is a visit to a museum in Vancouver full of masks of Northwestern tribal peoples; there is a voyage to Germany which includes a screening of World War II and Holocaust footage. These arenas are presented overlappingly; happening in mind time they are all of a fabric. The poem contains towards its end, in large bold letters, the ambiguous word "DISARM," and the boast "I sang him down," for that is what the female singers of love's trials do: disarm the audience and sing the bad feelings away. This is a fitting message to end with, a known but profound thing to say, but the life circumstance from which the section springs, the betrayal by her lover, remains unresolved in the book. Both books end in an unanticipated personal disaster. The divorce at the end of Book I necessitates the tonal change of Book II, which is lonelier, perhaps harsher, less full of letters from men. Book II must also deal more with death and illness, being the book of a now middle-aged person.

As pervasive as the poet's own life drama in the poem is a sense of a political world, national and international, tugging at her for constant response. The poem is about love and war, just like an epic, but love includes the love between parent and child, and war does not include participation or firsthand knowledge. War is the distress of observation, never combat or suffering; the author, being a woman and an American, has never seen a war, has only been as close to it as her father's participation in the European theater of operations in the 1940s, before she was born. On the other hand the equipment of war is everywhere about her: Waldman cofounded and still teaches at the Naropa Institute in Boulder, Colorado, next door to Rocky Flats and its plutonium plant, and her immediate community is always aware of the environmental danger of that element. The United States may not be under any threat of war, but the newspapers are still full of descriptions of new kinds of weapons (there are lists of these throughout *Iovis*), as the video games Ambrose plays are all about combat and weapons. The United States is forever catching up to its war in Vietnam; there are the Gulf War, the ethnic war in ex-Yugoslavia, other wars about the globe to keep track of and react to. Waldman's reactions vary from citizen's letters to spells and chants designed to "sing down" the spirit of war; the image of the poet is of someone all-sensitive and ever-vigilant, though powerless in the conventional senses. The whole self is given over to interaction with "what's happening," but it all takes place on the page or stage, in the spirit or imagination. No other setting is possible. Wald-man presents, especially in performance, a sort of symbolic figure, a theatrically triumphant force. "I sang him down" and then "I rang him down," her having sung and rung down in *Iovis* the masculine ego's will to power, is a boast that isn't true, for nothing ever gets sung down by anyone, certainly war doesn't. On the other hand if one is moment by moment singing against such power, inside such moments, the power is sung down. And if everybody participated in such singing down . . . ?

There may be initially irritating aspects of *Iovis;* I find that fa-miliarity with the voice of the poem, really giving oneself over to it, alleviates the irritation. Since the poem is built on the pre-sentation of a person and her life, one accepts the poet finally as a friend, gets used to her "faults," and comes to enjoy her com-pany. One may at first think the heads self-aggrandizing and nineteenth century in tone; after a while one just reads them, takes them for granted like anything a friend does that you wouldn't dream of doing. Parts of the poem may feel thin; I think that is built into the genre, parts of *Maximus, Paterson,* and the *Cantos* feel a little thin to me—as well as garrulous, corn-pone, flowery, forced, self-indulgent, pretentious, and impene-trable. The form makes flaws possible; possibly poetry should make room for flaws, being a human form. There are other kinds of flaws in other kinds of poetry: stuffiness, coldness, the omission of nearly everything we think about. Poets like Wald-man, her close friend the late Allen Ginsberg, and Williams him-self have sometimes had trouble getting the critical appreciation they deserve, as if to be unpreciously in life can never coexist with being intellectual, "smart enough." Williams as far as I can tell is still not taken for an intellect: his acceptance by the main-stream tends to be an excuse for more prose-in-verse descrip-tions of objects, yards, and animals. It seems to me that Waldman has evolved from the earlier modernist epic her own form based on an acute observation of life's form, how things come and go around. Unlike those of her predecessors, her epic is based on the intellectually sophisticated tenets of Buddhism. Buddhism, like politics and the personal, infuses the books. It provides an ethical and philosophical base for much of Waldman's stance, certainly supporting her rejection of a god outside the mind, a Jove, and even supporting the "random" form of the book: "I will tell you about the Buddhist approach to cause & effect. There is no first cause, there is no final cause" (XXIII, from Book I). Buddhism is embedded, after some twenty-five years of practice, in her mind and in her daily activity, Buddhist terminology supplies detail and color of language, Buddhist ceremony sometimes supplies the shape of a section. For example, section XIV of Book II, "One Taste," is a scored performance based on a Buddhist meditation to the point that "all experience & phenomena have the same inherent quality of energy, whether it be negative or positive, painful or pleasureable":

TEAR YOU OUT OF ME!

long long enough
rub together the deceptive existence
of me & other

(*rubs hands together*)

TEAR YOU OUT OF ME!

You exist because you do not exist.
Other

I taste my hand
All two of them, salty

I extend them to the mountains & the sea

(bends over, rocking from side to side
licking both hands). . . .

If one and the other, mountain and sea and crackpot nation, all taste the same, if I am the other, surely a simple harmony is possible between us, between all that is. If war has the same taste as peace, why bother with something so costly?

Waldman uses mythology, all sorts of mythologies, somewhat differently from her modernist forebears. For her it is less of a narrative or way of participating in the ongoing ancient stories. Sometimes myth is a way of confronting serious moments, is connected with performance not just of a poem but of a dangerous time. Through identification with mythical figures one can rise high enough above events to take them calmly and even perform potentially curative ritual. Myth is a proper place to pray and hope from. In section XXII of Book II, "Cosmology: Within the Mind of the Sleeping God," Waldman concentrates on the figure of Bernadette Mayer (a poet and Waldman's close friend) lying comatose in a hospital bed after having had a stroke. Mayer becomes the Hindu deity Vishnu, the "sleeping god," supported by the nine-headed serpent Ananta, the tubes which surround her body in the bed. The seeming danger of the coma, which has been induced by the doctors themselves to protect the patient, recedes; the fearfulness the occasion invokes in Waldman is overcome by making the events exalted, cosmic (as they likely are); at the end of the poem Mayer "abides in the nursery of young stars . . . studded with stars she sleeps."

But the most obvious mythic figure used throughout *Iovis* is the title figure, though the adventures and deeds of the Roman god are never invoked. Jove is a concept, a key to meditation on the world's condition, and a means of praising and attacking the masculine *without* getting personal. The title of course speaks to the word "Maximus," but whereas Olson identifies with Maximus, Waldman can never be Jove, and the irony of the title is in its necessary lack of egoism. We are back at the beginning of my essay. Can a woman have an ego, can a woman poet get away with having an ego? Waldman's poem is directly involved with the ego question, as she is determined both to be allowed an ego by society and also to find a means to transcend it, a double process which seems to be as cyclical as everything else in the poem. How can one be oneself, and at the same time how can one care for others—all others, female and male? Myth is used in the search for harmless and healing ways to be grand, and in the search for ways to free oneself from the quotidian, as we are expected to live it in a society grown away from myth and religion. In fact Olson uses myth to the same end of deepening and sacralizing a "personal" territory, his Gloucester, which is in danger of trivialization. Any good poet recommits life to its full depth, nowadays in the face of great odds since depth is denied in favor of genetics, economics, the thin images produced by the great variety of new machines. As everyone would seem to know but doesn't really, the images of myth and of poetry aren't limited by the dimensions of what we literally see and hear: the mind holds them almost without the senses, and so they are potentially as enormous as all there is. That is the wisdom of Olson's epic, and of Waldman's.

# Lorenzo Thomas

## *A Private Public Space*

In a lecture, "The Blues and the King's English," delivered at the Naropa Institute in 1989 and printed in the anthology *Disembodied Poetics* (1994), Lorenzo Thomas discusses the difference between "court" poetry and "public" poetry. He explains that the former tradition evolved from European courts, was transplanted to the United States by poets such as Anne Bradstreet, was further utilized by those such as Emily Dickinson, and is now in the hands of any contemporary poet who writes for the limited educated world of poetry readers or for her/himself. Public poetry, by contrast, exemplified somewhat by Beat poetry but much more by the work of, say, the Harlem Renaissance poets or the Black Arts poets (with whom Thomas is associated), purports to fulfill a community function, representing a community's ideas or feelings. The poems come from, and are delivered back to, the street or the common space/mind of the community. (The court was a very different kind of community that encouraged "individual" poetry.)

Thomas's exegesis is, as usual, clear and amusing—learned, down-to-earth, and useful to the Naropa audience of potential professionals who would not necessarily understand the connection between specific poetries and specific audiences. Thomas is saying, Don't complain that they don't listen to your poetry in the mall if you're not truly speaking to and for the mall—and you're obviously *not,* because you're not down at the mall right now; you're here at this special school of poetics and Buddhist studies.

With regard to Thomas's own poetry, this advice is useful but

From *Poetry International,* no. 1 (1997).

also problematic. A definitive division of poetry into court and public types no longer seems true; there are other poetries, a spectrum of practice between those two words or worlds, including Thomas's own. For Thomas has invented a form that allows for an innovative coincidence of the public and the private. And were poets like Bradstreet and Dickinson really some species of court poet? What difference did it make whether a woman was a "court" or "public" poet, since there was neither court nor public for her? What "special" audience might there have been for a Puritan poet in a minuscule colony? If Emily Dickinson wrote primarily for herself, what is the meaning of those lines "This is my letter to the World / That never wrote to Me—"? Isn't Dickinson supposed to have been greatly influenced by that most public of forms, hymns? And Dickinson was always speaking to the future—she didn't throw her poems away, she put them in a trunk. Many people on the street and in the mall know them now. My point is threefold: first, that poets often have an indistinct idea of who they're addressing as audience; second, that there are many overlapping audiences; and third, that the future may contain the poet's real audience, even though the poet is responding to the present's pressures. Lorenzo Thomas's approach to the "problem" of audience is a sculpted monolithic fusion of courtly and public tradition through the medium of an immaculate line. For the courtly line and the public line are both immaculate (in the lecture, among his examples of each tradition are Sir Philip Sidney and the blues): the lines of Bradstreet and Dickinson are not.

Thomas's "early" poem "Wonders," written in an uncharacteristic consistently short line (and uncharacteristically "personal") is both a masterpiece by itself and an indication of how impeccable Thomas's line will be, with its exact weighting of each word and consistence of pace. The nervous erratic possibilities, the way a music might freak out of where it was and become quasi-uncontrolled buzz or twitter or screech, will not be part of this poetry. There will be changes of pace in future poems, but these changes of pace will be strictly controlled: Thomas is a genius at taking his time. "Wonders" was written in the early seventies, while Thomas was serving in Vietnam, and conveys a "simple" nostalgia for New York and Harlem:

Sometime I wonder.
Will I ever hear
*Nostalgia in Times Square*
Again, in some Avenue B
Break-in 1/2 bath flat
Will I ever sit
In the sun, high
On a Lenox terrace
And watch the Harlem River run
Away from the dope and the crime
To the gray East
Again? And me
With some Boone's Farm
Meaning no harm
On anybody
Sitting there digging
Eddie Palmieri's
Hip conversations
With Obatala.

—from *The Bathers*

The details, the musical and geographical references, "Boone's Farm" (a cheap fruit wine), as well as the Lower East Side tenement, feel particular to the poet's own experience but are in no way exclusive. This poem appears to be personal expression; but it is also a "public" poem that speaks for the black soldier caught in the Vietnam War and missing home. But it speaks for me as well, because I had a white Southwestern brother who served in Vietnam, though "Wonders" doesn't even mention Vietnam, except beneath the poem in the traditional "time and location" spot, where it says "Saigon/VNCH." The question of who a poem speaks for is complex, and Thomas's poems show us how complicated the notion of audience may become. This is *both* a private and a public poem, as exemplified in the way it sounds both like a song (public) and like a (particular) man talking; the inconsistency of the rhymes accentuates this fact.

A later (from the late seventies) poem in a longer line, "MMDCCXIII1/2," shows that Thomas's work has come to contain fewer proper names, fewer blatantly specific details, fewer references to "I," while keeping a feeling of personal circumstance that melts into the general so that you're not sure which is which. I'll quote this one in full:

> The cruelty of ages past affects us now
> Whoever it was who lived here lived a mean life
> Each door has locks designed for keys unknown
>
> Our living room was once somebody's home
> Our bedroom, someone's only room
> Our kitchen has a hasp upon its door.
>
> Door to a kitchen?
>
> And our lives are hasped and boundaried
> Because of ancient locks and madnesses
> Of slumlord greed and desperate privacies
>
> Which one is madness? Depends on who you are.
> We find we cannot stay, the both of us, in the same room
> Dance, like electrons, out of each other's way.
>
> The cruelties of ages past affect us now
>                                    —from *Chances Are Few*

This poem raises the question, who is "us," who does the "our" refer to really? "We find we cannot stay, the both of us, in the same room": is this a couple, the poet and his lover, is this the poet and his reader? I know quite well the kind of apartment referred to, a piece of a tenement which has been divided up into the smallest possible apartments, with, at some time in the past, doors and locks inserted within the small territories to insure privacy within families or groups, exploited immigrants often, who must room together. "We" cannot, even with the locks off in later times, stay near each other, cautious and private, knowing from history and our own pasts that we might be cruel to each other. Such an apartment is itself a cruelty. The apartment, the poem states, is a metaphor for the way lives and minds are compartmented, are made out of past cruelties, are made mad. The poem is also musical, containing an echo of a villanelle. Is it a public poem? You can't imagine it being "used" by a "group," as Claude McKay's sonnet "If We Must Die," a poem protesting lynching, was used by both Winston Churchill during World War II and rioting prisoners at Attica in the seventies. Thomas's poem weds an intimacy—its hint of two people brushing past each other—to a larger general message. It's a new kind of poem, a new way of thinking in a poem, where the specific and the general coincide because the specific really is specific but isn't allowed to tip the poem's balance towards itself. The emotion in the poem is clean, neither politically over-dramatic nor romantically pointing towards self. The tone is sad, exasperated, but curiously warm. There is something like a new kind of emotion here, communal and private at once. This is partly because Thomas isn't fictionalizing: it's a real apartment (in a Langston Hughes poem, for example, it wouldn't be). The "we" is somewhere between two and a community, not locked up in the communal (as it would be in a poem, say, by Amiri Baraka). Nor is the political content something that must be partly excavated from beneath the quotidian (as in a poem of Frank O'Hara's). Both communal and personal seem up-front at once, as if the poet is fully conscious of his identity in both worlds.

Thomas's later poetry is characterized by a number of long-lined and long, jazz-like pieces with unpredictable repetitions and extended cadences; the subject tends to be "simple," racial oppression is a simple fact, but the treatment, like jazz, is complicated, producing its own refined logic and a large, flexible capacity to amuse. In "The Blues and the King's English," Thomas says that there is a "part of the courtly tradition which . . . has to do with the question of amusing oneself. And of course the word *amusement* means just what it says: being touched by the muses." Thomas insists on his own amusement while composing, on his right to enjoy what he is doing. Such an attitude obviously precludes the simple delivery of a message. And in the case of translation it even seems to preclude a simple translation: Thomas's translations are "adaptations" rather than translations. His adaptation, for example, of the French Guyanese poet Léon Damas's famous "Hiccups" is utterly loose, hilarious, and fresh:

> When you lift your nose do it right!
> . . . . . . . . . . . . . . . . . . . . . . . . . . . .
> My mother, Mom
> Taught her son memorandums
> . . . . . . . . . . . . . . . . . . . . . . . .
> In your "drum battle" with Otis,

Otis
who hasn't even made a comeback
from his
baptism
Can't even speak French    dig it?
—from *Chances Are Few*

Thomas believes, again from "The Blues and the King's English," that there is no such thing as "anonymous folk creation." Rather he believes "all poems are produced by some force out there which then focuses on some individual to collect the sounds and words." This is not, in current critical jargon, to privilege the poet; it is a job description which implies keeping oneself attuned to large forces. It privileges those forces, whether ineffable and musical, or sociopolitical, or what's more likely some combination of them.

Thomas's longer works present a "speaker" who is one among others. He speaks both for and to, and is not individualized, in the sense that a personal life is delineated, but he is the sole maker of the poem's music and logic. His poems are thoughtful, and thoughtfulness is an individual (one-at-a-time) quality. Looking, then, at the ten-plus-page work "Class Action" (in *Chances Are Few*), one sees a poem which, after an initial comparison of African Americans to wallpaper, and a passage in the radio-dedication genre ("To Junior and Susie, Diana with her fine self," etc.), begins definitively in the "we" mode: "We spat on the groundlings from there" (the balconies where blacks were kept segregated in "the movie houses of the plains"); "We chewed the Jujubes before we hurled them." But also "We are the wallpaper":

> We are the wallpaper fraying
> Out of woodwork anchors
> We are asking questions and question answers
> Too vague to be forgotten for their haste

Five pages into the poem, having been speaking about wallpaper, about the emptiness of movies and their images and of a movie-like life, and about the fact that "Nobody gives a damn what niggers say," Thomas says, "What shall I do but speak":

If I should speak, the wallpaper would break
Its silence, too.
Should I despite some fiction of myself
To talk, as the wallpaper should?
Should I forget myself because spirits are talking
Or pleas to you or yourself or your master
When, obviously, no plea does no good
And any plea at all does little better
Than simply being there, like the woodwork;
Working yourself up like wallpaper.

And then a few lines later:

As strategy, it isn't logical a bit
But if it works, it's a breakthrough to logic.

Unlettered negroes call this logic Jazz

The poem has previously invoked mythological Africa with its hordes of pouting-lipped juju spirits who would speak through one, making a logic, a song to hurl down on the heads of the whites, as those in the segregated balconies hurled down Jujubes, a favored movie candy of the fifties, hard pellets in bright colors. This poem is then a power speaking, a song, a thoughtful musical expanse, with nothing new to say, in a sense, but all words are new if inspired. It ends on a note of "I," comes down hard on the speaker in the end, on "I":

And I'm a lie! Because I see in twos or threes
Because my view is amplified by night
Crazily flies into the dawning sun
Cussing & fussing like it supposed to bes
A natural man
Because my spirit slaps me upside my head
And makes me turn to see the others pouting
Because by lack of eloquence
I'm left here to embarrass you by shouting
That we must speak or be like patterns on a wall. . . .

It would be more of a lie not to name oneself "I"; the singer is not "we" and must take responsibility for what he says. The very last lines are: "You don't have to take my word / For 'it.'"

Thomas's poems are self-consciously musical and are also about music. Music dissolves borders between existing logical and existential compartments. It elevates "things" to a more sublime flow, a possibly superior thinking that jumbles whatever together, as one's own daily mind does, but making a framework for, a precision of, actuality. In music a different kind of sense gets made; and music applied to poetry will not necessarily result in an easily explicable thing. In a more recent poem of Thomas, "Excitation" (from the anthology *From the Other Side of the Century* [1994]), the reader is initially unsure of everything except the fact that she/he is inside of a musical structure. As in life the elements of the poem don't seem entirely to match or mesh, except by being together. Music makes the poem work because, as the poem states at its conclusion, music is useful when "the words fail," being a different kind of logic. "Excitation" begins with a diction which satirizes a sort of antiquated cornball "white" literary mode:

> Oh wondrous thing it is
> Oh what a wondrous thing it is
> We often thought, to live
> Through the senses
> When they quicken and stir at even

Subsequently that quaint tone begins to break, in a difficult stanza which begins "When nature struggles against artifice"; and Thomas goes on to speak of sense impressions which get stored, forgotten, and much later unwrapped and puzzled over: "Where did this stuff come from!" One is reminded of "MMDCCCXIII 1/2" and how it speaks of a drag from the past into the present and future. In this poem, though, Thomas seems to be talking about "stuff," not "cruelty" but the accumulation in general of garbage in the memory and psyche. This is particularly the sound of white cultural garbage: "When natural struggles against artifice / In a madly sensuous pas de deux / Lovely as the chevrons of late traffic." Then, in a "wake-up" section in uppercase letters, we are told that all of this is an excerpt from a dream:

> A SPECIAL SORT OF MUSIC IN THE AIR . . . SOMETHING
> THAT WAKES YOU UP
> JUST LIKE SUNLIGHT

> LIKE A PHONECALL AT DAWN
> 15 MINUTES BEFORE THE ALARM GOES OFF
> A ROUGH AND ROLLING MUSIC
> LIKE THE 1940'S BLUES
> WHISKEY & WOMEN AND ALL THE OTHER JIVE
> THE JIVERS KNEW

So the reader is led to a meditation on the music of rhythm and blues great Charles Brown ("all of these cats / were Charles / yes, even / Nat 'King' Cole"), and the racist milieu of the forties. This music, these times too, are given a "garbagey" characterization: "sordid ordered trash," "pulp days, pulp times," "shoofly." The poem then riffs out on the sound of that music ("The permutated sounds / of a special estranged English"):

> Byebye, bye
> Baby
> byebye
> Oh what a wondrous thing
> I think it is
> But goddam baby
> baptist to the heart
> I'm getting tithed of you, momma
> But I love, Lord knows
> most as much as I loves
> myself

The section lengthens, taking on more words and phrases for repetition, becoming more and more musical: "moaning and going on," "fool," "in the background," "in the wildwood," church music as well as profane pop being dragged into the argument, which begins to feel very complex in tone. The music is great but is also "pulpy": later to be relegated to forgotten sense impressions, as a whole time, a whole suffering culture itself might be. The music is that of an estranged people, and because it is "rough and rolling" it incites its oppressors to violence against its practitioners. The music makes its listeners foolish because it keeps them from thinking: "Certainly this should awaken the mind / And the senses should shut down in shame."

But how could one, the speaker says, "shoo this shoofly away" when music is "such a lovely break in the day"? At the end of the release into pure song, that voice returns to make a pointed speech:

> So much to say, we negroes here
> Oh yes, we've had some fun
> Have sang the blues and did what had to be done
> We often thought, to live
> O what a wondrous thing
> Fleeting to sight yet permanent
> To sit despised on the outskirts of your town
> Black fat deprived and jap-eyed
> Yes, we sing. "Bbaby baby baby, why you?"

Lines from earlier in the poem are at this point rushing in to assume different and heavier meanings from before, for example:

> When nature struggles against artifice
> To be unwrapped some day when bullshit fails
> . . . . . . . . . . . . . . . . . . . . . . . . . . . . . . . . . . .
> Lovely as the chevrons of late traffic
>> So Prussian so precise
>> Like a phonecall at dawn from your baby

The poem ends reaffirming the specific importance of a Charles Brown and "a rough and rolling music":

> To be unwrapped someday
> When words fail
> What use they serve
> Or else they wouldn't have been
> Singing

Brown's music is vindicated, as is a time and a culture. This poem is finally an amalgam of anger, playfulness, protest, history; it makes a large meaning because it implies paradoxically that any culture's specifics and sufferings both will be forgotten and are real right now. Like all major poetry, it changes continually on rereading, because it's as complicated as the person who's written it: its aim isn't simplicity, the exclusion of some feelings and thoughts for purposes of emphasis. Instead Thomas creates a new cognition, that is, a knowing, a piece of mind-experience, of thinking and sensing ("think" and "sense" being important, dichotomized words in the poem). This new cognition is held in place by a music adopted from jazz and popular forms and from poetic forms involving repetition of lines.

It would be remiss to write of Lorenzo Thomas's work without mentioning the felicities of his technical talent. Several consecutive stanzas from the middle of the lovely poem "The Gods' Own Privilege" (from SCARLET, no. 2 [Fall 1990]) will illustrate the subtleties of his practice:

> Shadows of lavalites
> Syncopated dance of golden palms
> Methedrine gospel breakdown
> Echoes of Lydian song
>
> Would there be thunderbolts,
> Would there be lightning
> The long slow freight with its careening lamp,
> A ponderous rumble following
> Pathway of the spark, going on
> Three four hundred miles
>
> Remembering thin nights in Colorado
> The night we lay on the banks of the Same
> River, afraid to go in
> Would there be lightning
> Would the next step take us
> Vanishing
> Into the pearl gray sky
>
> The would be thunder weights each
> Corner of the sky

This poem begs to be read aloud, and when it is the syllables are delicious and the lines, subtly shifting in length, a pleasure to lay against one another. I find such qualities hard to discuss without dryness. The mysterious word "lavalites" in its genitive phrase, followed by a longer more ornate genitive phrase, followed by a short "beatnik" noun-jam: "Methedrine gospel breakdown," and then the evocation of the Greek musical mode (the poem is addressed to "Lydia") in the last line of that stanza: all of this indicates a remarkable ear, but Thomas isn't showing off; he's succumbing to the beauty of what he hears. In the second of those stanzas, the two lines beginning with "Would there be" both ask a conditional question and manage to make the "would's" be volitional as well, "would" in the sense of "I hope." That added nuance gives the lines weight and passion. Rhyming "following" and "going on" is wonderful. The third stanza contains the strange phrase "thin nights," and the exactly right "we lay on the banks of the Same / River," and the not-at-all-overplayed return of "would." The notion that the thunder weights the corners of the sky makes sense immediately—the sound the thunder makes in the immense Colorado sky is solid rather than threatening. It is "The Gods' Own Privilege" to speak like this. The spirits of poetry "inspire," they whisper in the poet's ear as he/she writes down what they say, in whatever tradition.

ॐ

I've used the word "new" often and emphatically in this essay, because I think there is a new kind of poetry mind at work here. It isn't antipathetic to the personal; rather one feels as if it's guarding, rightly, its privacy while letting the feel of that privacy through. It uses personal feeling and knowledge to achieve a public voice that's thoughtful enough, playful and subtle enough, to appeal to a reader or audience member as an individual intelligence without separating her/him from others, from communal issues. The articulating of this voice is an important achievement. It corresponds to what many people are when not pushed to extremes by outrageous cultural demands: reasonable, musical, both gregarious and private. This voice doesn't exhort, it just talks. Speaks. "What shall I do but speak?" Speaking means both speaking out and just speaking because humans talk. Humans talk and make poems and sing and play musical instruments. They do these things in every culture, "naturally."

Lorenzo Thomas's poetry often exemplifies a natural reaction to an unnatural stress. But it's not just reaction; Thomas's poetry insists on the primacy of making poetry as a natural activity. One may be protesting but one is simultaneously making something, as a way of being in a life that continuously asserts its temporality. One has to be in that life, not merely protest it, or deliver a message as if the point-blank urgency of the message can fill up all of time. This is an obvious thing to say, but how much of poetry shows that its making is as important as its message, that it amused the writer to write it, and to that extent amuses the reader because both writer and reader are alive with real hours to fill? A poem may not change the world right away, but it will *be,* and thus change, the time of those who read or perform it for as long as the performance lasts.

# Douglas Oliver's New York Poem

*Penniless Politics,* a long poem by the British poet Douglas Oliver, could be called a quintessentially New York poem, if by "New York poem" were understood the result of necessary changes in that genre in the late 1980s and early 1990s. Under the pressures of deregulated capitalism and multinationalism, multiculturalism and immigration, an attempt to write seriously in and of New York could only result in something different from predecessor poems. Serious predecessors would include poems by Whitman, Crane, and Ginsberg, as well as poems by the various generations of the New York School, which I have recently defined as successive groups of poets responsive in their writing to New York as a community and as an international city. As a community New York is still unique, still that in-your-face place where you are free to do what you want but are also accountable to strangers for it, are anonymous but never alone. As an international city New York is simply an example, one of many which reflect the moment's economic and cultural forces, complications, paradoxes—all those fuzzy words which any poem would ignore in order to tell what's going on.

Oliver lived in New York on the Lower East Side between roughly 1987 and 1992, having previously lived in various English cities and then in Paris, and having recently written a poem called *The Infant and the Pearl,* a satire on Thatcher's England, the new England, based exactly on the rigorous verse requirements of the medieval poem *The Pearl.* Oliver's theory was that if a political satire were written in a form such as that of *The Pearl,* it would be dignified and permanent as well as satirical, with the kicker being *The Pearl*'s rigid use of alliteration. (Alliteration in Oliver's poem

Review of *Penniless Politics* (Newcastle upon Tyne, U.K.: Bloodaxe Books, 1994). From *Chicago Review* 15, no. 1 (1999).

turns out to be loopy: dreamy and jokey and lacy.) The poem was a great success in England. By not writing from England but from France, Oliver had distance enough to see before other poets how England had changed; moving to New York he perceived the same forces at work there when (believe me) hardly anyone else did. Bogged down in a life in one's city, one often sees it in the way of the art of ten, twenty years ago; the movies sometimes keep up better by depicting the world as it looks, but are always constructed around the same perfectly stupid stories. Poets often aren't looking because they're looking inside themselves; it's rare to catch a moment when things are changing. Oliver's *Penniless Politics* catches its moment in detailed accuracy, through an unusual and deliberately idealistic story, but it's fun.

*Penniless Politics* abounds with tenements and streets, references to the likes of "Leona" and a Sharptonesque Reverend, the Rainbow Coalition, crack (refigured as the ultimate drug Behemoth), and recognizes the arrival of new immigrants, as exemplified in the takeover by Koreans of bodegas and corner stores. That is its moment, though its real moment is the future since the new immigration was and is just starting. The poem is set in a moment of transition when New York once again appears to be crumbling, downsliding from some previous glorious era into a dirty chaos, an inferior monument full of a more ordinary vitality than that of "the arts" (New York and its painting, architecture, literature patronized by its elite and often celebrated by New York poets). In *Penniless Politics* New York means a lot of immigrants trying to get by, a lot of loud and lively people grubbing for money. The form of the poem is meant to sound like the streets, like New York speech, and a bit like rap: an eight-line stanza—modified from Tasso's *ottava rima*—with end-rhymes and internal rhymes, long talky lines that turn surprisingly:

> All politics the same crux: to define humankind richly.
> No one non-populist or penniless can found a viable party
> though most religions have such saints. She was his Haitian
> saint Emen—Emen for Marie Noelle—for non-Christian
> Mary-Christmas. In New York with him, her husband, Will Penniless,
>     they'll found their party in a poem. Black with White nation,
> Voodoo-Haitian with immigrant Anglo-Scots, hairy-chesty,
> penniless. Mrs. Penniless, with him, Will Penniless.

The eight-liners are broken up by other forms including set pieces for Will, a poet, purported newspaper articles, and certain political documents.

The plot of the poem turns about the founding and progress of a new political party, called Spirit, without power or money. Invitations to the party's first meeting, instigated by Emen, a Haitian immigrant, and Will, an Anglo-Scots immigrant, are by chain letter. Crucial members of the party, the poem's characters, include Hispanic Dolores Esteves, a Cuban boxer named High John, African American Ma Johnson, a young Korean woman (Republican) named Yuhwa Lee, Juan her Hispanic boyfriend, the middle-aged Chinese man Peter Sung, and the Jewish lawyer Lou Levinson. They make politics and they also make love; Will and Emen, Yuhwa Lee and Juan, Peter Sung and Dolores, all couple rather graphically as the races do and will, producing more and more of those children who are unsatisfied by the racial categories they are allowed to select from on census forms. Spirit gets itself into the papers with theatrics and hints of Voodoo, recruits members in tenements, and finally receives some real financing through High John's talents as a boxer when he becomes "the new light heavy champ of the whole freaking world!" Spirit then organizes a serious theatricalized event, a "ritual for a politics beginning again / in the breath of spirit," which involves members passing through a tunnel containing Voodoo tableaux and personages before confronting a sort of mirror and, finally, an altar with a book in which to write one's three choices for party policy. There is 98 percent unanimity that the party should work to "make material wealth for other people, spiritual wealth for ourselves"; that the "only qualification for party membership should be goodness and respect for the history and future of the people's individual families"; and that "Long-term earth environment issues must have first consideration to save resources that our children's children should inherit."

After that, Spirit proceeds to buy back a 'hood in the impoverished Morrisania section of the Bronx through five schemes: "the Drug Bust, the Drug Rehab, the Bank Scam, the Store Score, and the Yuppie Cream." By means of rather wacky events, small stores and respectable buildings are financed. And through High John's money a tenement becomes equipped with drug dealers, a bank, and a money launderer ("Madre Hubbard," really Dolores); members of Spirit bilk and then entrap, using a Wall of Women, the cream or scum of the 'hood's dealers of the drug Behemoth. Then the press find out about the illegal bank and the money-laundering scheme and High John's and Dolores's names are tarnished; finally one night during a boxing match High John is assassinated by an unknown gunman and vitriol is thrown in Dolores's face. At High John's funeral—an emotional and populous occasion—Emen speaks with the aid of a voice box, which provides, as in Voodoo possession, the voice of a "rider." This rider uses the pronoun "esh" (possessive form "sher") to describe her/him/itself and declares, "I am Hooman." The Hooman announces that a new Constitution of the United States has now been written, then a "Declaration" is read, and the Constitution itself is sent to TV and radio stations in the form of computer disks containing only Hooman's oral version of the document. After this the A1 Congressional District (an imaginary district incorporating parts of the Bronx and Brooklyn) secedes from the United States, holding its own election in Prospect Park: Emen is elected president and Dolores vice-president. Other elections, all lightning-rapid events which end as soon as the election takes place, are held all over the country for about a year; but finally the party and the poem vanish into their ideal, and the poet turns on the reader and on himself in the poem's final line: "We wouldn't know Spirit if, Spirit on top, it fucked us up the ass."

What is this penniless politics like, as politics? If it's an ideal politics, it's ideal to an American moment circa 1990 and its incontravertible set of circumstances, its givens. That is, the poem's not set in a utopia, it's not a depiction of how people might behave in some deserted landscape or on another planet; though comic it's not fantastic. Actually, every detail of it is possible; it's just that it wouldn't happen, and if it did happen, as the poem makes clear at its end, it wouldn't be enough. There is no ultimate proposal, no clear solution in an ever more corrupt world which is, to begin with, ruled by the friction between a conception and what takes place. What is Oliver's ideal given the circumstances? From the above plot summary one might suppose that he wishes for a politics rich in theatricality, in symbolism and ritual, that not being the same as religion but instead both playful and deep. It's partly the dryness and hypocrisy of political process that turns us Americans away from it, the drabness of the suits that the (still mostly) men wear, the insistence on lip service by people in high office to outmoded religious practices, the clichéd rhetoric, the necessary show of Victorian decorousness by presidential families (the First Lady must never Work), the lack of powerful symbols and of connection with *scary* forces. What if the president of the United States had to talk to the keeper of the Delphic Oracle from time to time, someone who breathed mephitic vapors and spoke in urgent obscurities? What if he had to face the gods before he decided policy?

Oliver's depiction of the meditative process leading to the formulation of Spirit's policy is of a confrontation with the gods which is performed by every member of Spirit, not just by its leaders. The meditation is both funny—fun—and gut-wrenching. We are taken through the process in the person of Ma Johnson, who begins by kneeling to think in a converted portable toilet. (I've recently read a life of a Byzantine saint who chose to meditate in such a place—it's quite traditional.) She concentrates on her life, on the painful deaths she's witnessed, on someone close to her addicted to drugs, on the uselessness of the speeches of black politicians. Then she enters a tunnel, having spoken the password "Ouvray biyaay poor mwon" (in an American accent, what one says in Creole to Legba, the Voodoo god of crossroads: "Open the gate for me"), and passes party members dressed as Voodoo gods: Baron Samedi, the god of cemeteries, who sits presiding over photographic images of roses and graves, and Erzulie, the bridal goddess who offers Ma Johnson wedding cake. After eating it

> . . . She rose and walked on, remembering the day
> of her own wedding but wrongly: she a burlesque bride
>     ushered

> along a deserted aisle to marry that woman,
> call her Mary, Emen, Erzulie, someone not quite human
> but large like her own soul. Down the corridor ahead
> the exit now glimmered grey as all other lights cut dead
> and walking towards the grey screen she saw an image
> of herself approaching, waddling the way she had, a dead

spitting image in the same clothes, mimicking her every
   movement.
She passed straight through the screen, straight through her
   own image

as a curtain of silvered threads, that is, the "screen," drifted
over her face and a whirring video camera clicked and
   stopped.

Ma Johnson proceeds down a ramp to straddle a coffin sticking
out of an altar, surrounded by icons, Buddhas, emblems of various religious, "a Toltec calendar . . . a Humanist lapel badge, a
philosophy book," etc. Specifically, she straddles a holographic
cross symbolizing the connection between upper and lower
worlds and from this position writes her policy choices in the
book on the altar.

As far as practicalities go, the poem proposes a goal beyond
conventional radical politics with its violent righteousness and
its ideals that arouse little popular interest, and beyond conventional liberal politics which serves the comfortable. It proposes
in Spirit a union of the qualities and beliefs that the immigrants
naturally bring with them: the fiery neighborhood activism of
Dolores, but also the usefulness of High John's earnings from
an ethically flawed form of entertainment, Yuhwa Lee's Republican knowledge of how to foster small businesses through Korean connections, Peter Sung's insistence on the value and hap-
piness of working for low wages. Capitalism can only be worked
with at this point, but wealth isn't an end in itself and needn't
be massive: wealth is how you help others and also how you keep
from being a burden on them. People like their neighborhood
lives and don't dream of becoming rich so much as of not having to worry about essential expenses. Will's particular contribution to Spirit is his energy and his poetry, which speaks of the
need for white males like himself to change, to give up their old
selves in order to get their selves back:

> . . . Give up my plummy fucker voice.
> Learn situation. Having left an English dream
> half-finished, come abroad
> seeking a voice change
> to find that my voice must

crack open like a snake's egg for,
being its old self, whole and ineffectual,
it takes part in the real only by irony.

*"Ah'm to suck your asshole, stomp it,*
*ain't mah style. You tell it, baby,*
*you fucking tell it, John, okay?*
*This is the play-off boy, you know it, I know it."*

In this politics, though, all must change their ideas of who
they are at least somewhat if all are to be included. That is the
meaning of the creature called the Hooman, Emen's rider, in
the crucial scene of High John's funeral:

. . . "My rider in me is complicated,"

came a femina perturba voice in English—rider being a
   usual
Voodoo term for the loa. "I'm not bisexual, but all-sexual,
he-she-she-he originating together in unique desires. Not
   African
desires, or Waspy ones, or Asian, or Hispanic, or
   Amerindian:
I contains all of esh, differences held separately, separate in
   unity,
held in each flash of personality like facets of the one
personality: think of a painting whose colors are individual
but simultaneously perceived, separate in brilliance, formal
   in unity."

Similarity between people must be sought as well as difference:
there is no politics without mutuality, without the Hooman as well
as the ethnic. This seems a simple enough principle, but a very
necessary multiculturalism has temporarily exploded the principle. Everyone has a difference and everyone has a problem:
dealing with all those differences and problems is impossible unless people are willing to stake a politics on *something* that's the
same. If it's just a legal notion of right or rights, that's too cold,
that doesn't get it, the society you can really be free in. Oliver always tends towards a notion of emotional warmth for his answers,
in other poems as in this one; with politics that seems right. Such
a warmth would not be perturbation or anger, righteousness, so
much as generosity and friendliness, the desire to help out.

Spirit's Declaration, a declaration of secession based straight-forwardly on the Declaration of Independence, states that District A1 is the poorest district in the United States, due to "historical circumstances of immigration and slavery" but also due to "the establishment of absolute political groupings," the military-industrial complex, and the American corporate and financial elite. The president of the United States is called "effectually a tyrant who, voted in by 20% of an electorate, supported in policy by Congressional majority representing little more than one third of the electorate, and—scantly heeding even that popular mandate but swaying a nation by lies and political manipulation—enters into a cabal with a few nearest friends, his own appointees, to commit our own hands to the bloody sacrifice of soldiers and civilians in foreign lands." (This poem was written at the time of the Gulf War.) Furthermore, the immense size of the United States is called detrimental to the needs of the individual. District A1 will therefore secede and follow the dictates of a new Constitution, whose preamble and whose major differences from the original Constitution of the United States are the next and nearly last matter of the poem. The new Constitution provides for, among other things: the establishment of three levels of Congress; the stripping of all but ceremonial powers from the president and vice-president; changes in the system of primary elections; a primacy of interest in the concerns of other nations and in the environment; a phasing out of nuclear armaments; a sure alliance with the United Nations; and changes in taxation including ensuring that "no private individual shall earn an average annual income of more than eight times the national average," with family holdings also to be severely limited.

In fact these purported constitutional changes pinpoint exact problem areas in American politics, things which *could* be changed, slowly and legally, through a will to change and an opening out towards other people and countries. Some of the changes are perhaps already taking place, but poetry's trajectory into the future can be a far one; it's possible that a poem's way of assisting in transformative processes (which is perhaps one of its major jobs) is always slower than one might suppose. The poem's reception in three forms of publication (as a temporary small-press pamphlet from Iain Sinclair's Hoarse Commerce imprint; as part of *The Scarlet Cabinet*, a compendium of books by both Oliver and myself; and finally as a book from Bloodaxe in England) has been generally favorable. It was well received by Oliver's neighbors in New York, members of the Lower East Side's white artistic community as well as the predominantly Hispanic and black audience at the Poet's Cafe (where Oliver tested excerpts in poetry slams), that is, by people who live the tenement life and share its problems. A few middle-class well-educated whites have called it racist, because its characters are of races other than the author's, because he makes speeches and dialogue for people of other races. After the foregoing description of the poem and the urgency of its concerns, such an objection seems prissy and misses the point. We must learn to speak each other's languages; we will not be allowed the luxury of extreme difference from each other in the future, unless we propose to be in a constant state of warfare. The future is about proximity and mixture; that is the real correctness behind political correctness. We are all right here, next to each other; we can't afford to turn away from each other on some grounds of impropriety.

Finally I would like to point out that I have been in dialogue with the poem's subject throughout this essay and have taken its technical prowess for granted. I've approached it through the story, as one approaches the works of Chaucer and Homer, and through the matter of it, as one approaches Dante. This isn't to argue that Oliver is as good as those authors—who cares about "as good as"? It's to say that this is another kind of poem from the ones I usually find myself talking or reading about; it's not just that it's narrative, it's that it doesn't draw attention to its technique (though if you concentrated on its sound and flow you might find yourself rather thrilled). One's rapport with the poem's subject is whole, and that quality is one that distinguishes it from *The Infant and the Pearl*, which uses technique to show that politics is worthy of treatment in a poem and that Thatcher's England is degraded in comparison with the architectonics and imaginary landscape of *The Pearl*. New York tends only to have a present, a present from which it's difficult to get any distance. To live there is to be in its story, which is perhaps why it isn't a stronghold of linguistically based poetry.

# Steve

The downstairs buzzer rings, Tom at the intercom. Then big feet, more than two, tromp upstairs, rush through door—excitement, Tom tall and blond and an even taller blonder bigger man who physically but not emotionally (I can tell) resembles a mountainous iceberg. Is attractive. I'm sorting a mass of laundry, and humiliatingly wearing the thick-lensed wire-rimmed glasses, because having a contact lens crisis. I'm also wearing my yellow Yellow Press t-shirt with the smoking (there's a cigarette in the mouth of the) fish, yuck. This is Steve, says Tom; it's his brother that's why he's so excited. They tromp on through to Ted's bed, it's a surprise, it's announced as one, that is that Steve has moved to New York. I follow, watching and listening to this unexpected being. Steve is wearing The Jacket, the one I will ever after associate with him, a sort of black plaid on a background of iceberg. He has a deep beautiful voice, from deep in a big chest. It's the voice (I will soon find out) that all his poems ride, they're conceived for that sound, fluid, changeable, playing . . . it will make up words for us, contribute permanently to our vocabulary— "You're making me crazy" not "driving me crazy"; "our teenage dad," the actor Harry Carey Jr. skulking off into rehab for a codeine habit at the age of fifty-something; "dad used to say, whose piece of meatloaf is that floating in the toilet?"; "Tom has l.s.i. today" (that's low self-image); "I'm queer for girls"; "Let me take you to dinner for Steve's Eve" (that's the night before his birthday); recitations of Kerouac reciting Railroad Earth— Steve's voice is made for it. An exact sense of rhythm, since Steve Carey is a drummer, like Clark Coolidge, but he also can sing and play the guitar, one song anyway, something about being blue (sings it at every party). Doesn't Tom once get him to

---

Delivered as a lecture at Naropa University (Summer 1998).

sing with him at the Ear Inn (before it goes totally Language Poetry) the song from the end of John Ford's *The Searchers* (in which
their (Steve and Tom's) father is butchered by the Comanches):
"What makes a man to ramble / What makes a ma-a-an to roam,
blah blah blah blah blah blah blah, and turn his back on home /
Ride away / Ride away / Ride awaaaaaaaaay"?

> "These are the times
> the elders spoke of"
> and you
> are simple and finally an expression
> of that presently remembered speed
>
> You have come halfway.—
> near as damnit, anyway
>
> There is a tribe
> that has to leave to learn
> You heard this young—
> kept it ordinary—
> flag in every wind
> —"Poem: To the Coast Indian," from *20 Poems*

Steve has left the West Coast at least partly to flee bad habits,
he has to get away from the places where he can easily score the
pills he by now needs. His habits seem large to me but he's one
of the biggest men I've ever known, though I've known other
large men who are poets; like theirs his sensibility is responsive
to every delicacy in words, but he is less jealous than most of
them—because he's literally and figuratively bigger?—less jealous, I mean, of others' poetic accomplishments. Instead he's instantly appreciative of their turns of phrase, he allows those into
his imagination, into his collection of choice lines to brood over
and entertain himself with interiorly or in the conversations we
all have about great lines. One of his own recent poems is "Mrs.
Murcheson" about an English woman who grants mysterious
(well not really) manner of favor to servicemen during The War:

> She was white like a sonnet
> in evening gray not premature.
> Unskilled at what she would confer

five afternoons, every moment matters now.
Many men in services. . . .
—from The Lily of St. Mark's

This is a find, a man who identifies with women, he is in many ways as passive as women are traditionally, he is wounded from adolescence but that's a secret he never tells me not the whole story, he adores his grandmother Ollie (Olive Carey, who acted in *The Searchers* and other films) and physically resembles her and his father (Tom resembles the grandfather, Harry Carey). I think, thinking now, he probably never hit anyone during his whole adulthood; so many large men never do; though he knew how to be scary with his size. The time several years later that he and Marion are living at our apartment, 101 St. Marks Place, and Jeffrey the downstairs S&M guy, a petulant gay cokehead, tiny, who hates for my children to be alive in the morning above his bed when he's hungover, rushes upstairs to complain because water's flooding down into his kitchen. Steve has taken some Valium and is bathing in the tiny tiny tub in the kitchen, his big body has made it to overflow; Jeffrey knocks, Steve answers the door, huge naked wet white from hair to toenail, a dripping Sasquatch or Yeti, and grins happily at Jeffrey. Jeffrey runs downstairs and never complains about anything again.

But that's pushing ahead. When Steve comes to town and moves in down the street on St. Mark's Place he's in despair and then in more despair; he's married to Effie whom he loves, a very small woman very coastal of the genre of that other coast. Effie comes to New York too and tries it for one week: there's a bitter cold snap on and furthermore the kitchen is filthy especially the stove, so Effie cleans the stove. Everyone sits around in the cold roach-infested apartment (what else does one do in December on the Lower East Side?) with the roach-infested stove on when the heat's off, talking, writing sometimes, play guitar. Steve, Tom, a girl roomie whose name I can no longer remember (who once cleaned my sink gratuitously, she was from California too) (Liz Palmer, I just found her name in Steve's poems), and Effie. Effie can't hack it; she tells me my collages remind her of art school (she is an artist but works for a burglar-alarm service, she draws horses). She bolts for California, the marriage is over even

119

though they love each other. And Effie gets to become a jockey in her new incarnation, that was her secret ambition. Steve is sad sad, loses weight. He needs to get a book out in order to cheer up Ted says, so Ted revives "C" Press once again and prints the slender volume called *The Lily of St. Mark's.* This title is after the song "The Lily of the West" (sung by Joan Baez, and also and not very well by Dylan) suggesting Steve's Westernness (he loves whitewall tires and smog and Ed Ruscha photos) and his pallor and esthetic purity (which Ted sometimes chides him for, as in Ted's line "Absolute quality tells absolutely nothing."). The cover by George Schneeman is a drawing of a generalized knave from a pack of cards, no special suit, unless lily ("lilies") could be construed as a suit. The knave holds something leaved which might be a lily. Inside there's a line drawing by George of Steve possibly emphasizing a quality of arrogance, well he has that too—many poets I know do. The poems' titles and dedications reflect influences and connections: Keith Abbott (with whom he coedited the glorious mag *Blue Suede Shoes,* but that's a whole other string of anecdotes, like the Gene Susquehanna parody letter submitting poems to *Blue Suede Shoes* and ending "P.S. I go down"), Jim Brodey (the poem's title "Blood Sugar" so oddly appropriate to Jim, Steve being a friend from Jim's days in California writing for *Creem* magazine), Phil Whalen from whom Steve has picked up certain sounds and architectonics—Phil is hero to us all, Ted Berrigan whom Steve constantly informs that his poem *AP,* which is "like" *Tambourine Life* and written after *Tambourine Life,* was composed without his knowing about *Tambourine Life.* The first poem is dedicated to me, imitates one of my imitations of the Chinese then turns into the first three lines of Kerouac's Railroad Earth:

### After Li Po (After Alice Notley)

Running dust, a light morning rain
Dark wet dust on window sills, freshened brickwork
Outside the city just awake
You call for another cup of coffee while I'm up
Well, old friend, I called you in from this storm
Leaving, please remember, that I too start soon
For this little alley in San Francisco
back of the Southern Pacific station at Third and Townsend
in redbrick of drowsy lazy afternoons

At the time I think it's surely not as good as my poem (Steve and I have quickly consented to sibling rivalry being born a month apart in the same year 1945); now I see it's all ear, the changes played on my poem "After Wang Wei" are subtle and brilliant as is the segue into little alley in San Francisco (always yearning for that coast, he always would ever after, though his love was really L.A., not San Francisco). Now Steve was not always in a great mood, or at least easy, and now that I've said that I won't have to bother with it again since everyone misses him and no one cares anymore about the pills (we did that too anyway) and the accompanying paralyses and needy needs; all that seems to remain is the feeling, the voice, shape, the sometimes toppled mountain (phrase I think I invented for him when he was in shattered mode). And obviously if he hadn't had his needy needs he wouldn't have been Steve. Another phrase of his: an intense nervous drug-related condition Sam Shepard calls the "openended shakes" (I think in *Tooth of Crime*) Steve says is better called the "whips and jangles." Is this true?

Meanwhile back in the chronology he is moving in with my best friend Marion, English like Mrs. Murcheson though more exotic and beautiful and certainly younger. He is cheering up, he is filling me in on his genius, his accomplishments, all the books he's already written, (unpublished) long things, *AP, The California Papers: AP* is 77 pages long and was written in 1967; *The California Papers* is 52 pages long and from around the same time, even earlier. They were conceived in isolation and a sort of serene desperation by a self-educated (was it a year of junior college?) very young (22 years old) genius? and is the genius part already over? He now seems to be involved in a Silver Poet sound. Only short works. There are also, but again in the past, the novels, a handful; I read one about an aviatrix named Elinor who is raped (I'm trying to remember the title—*The Absence of Their Surprise*); it's sad, characterized too by the white and beige colors that Steve likes so much, and is somehow a metaphor for something that's "happened" to Steve. He once makes Peggy stay up all night reading it after a workshop he's taught, reading it while he watches her. It was a sort of horrifying experience, Peggy says; Marion doesn't know where he is all night. My favorite of all these longer works is *AP* (but what difference does my preference make?):

During and after this time,
whatever is made of this
is in fact made, and so is
what came of it
which may be the same thing
but which has also made you
feel for something else,
and not just what was made of it,
nor, necessarily, something
entirely new or different
or, for that matter, old, familiar,
but something nonetheless,
that is if what I said was the truth.

—from *AP*

That passage only characterizes the performance aspect of the poem, which is, like *Tambourine Life*, made up as it goes along, in a way that involves several kinds of presentation, not just columnar but across the page, in dialogue, etc. With lots of references to TV. Steve watches lots of TV all of his life; *AP* reflects this for sure. But now what I'm remembering is . . . (this is not literary criticism, it's fonder than that) . . . how Steve calls any old sitcom episode a "work." "Don't you know this work?" (an episode of *The Odd Couple*). "It's the one where Oscar . . ." During their time together on St. Mark's Place, Steve and Tom are and watch *The Odd Couple*, they say; but then there's 7th St, where Marion and Steve first live together (watch TV together—the channels on Marion's decrepit black and white, inherited from Dick Gallup, are changed with nail clippers), some temporary apts, and finally 2nd Avenue, where Marion and Steve live in slightly more luxury with their son, Joe. Steve will be an excellent father, and I recently—in the real now present—made Peggy laugh a long long time by saying, "Men who forge Valium prescriptions make excellent fathers." I guess I'm laying myself open to charges of lack of seriousness, not serious enough about these grave matters: but people's drugs are subsumed into all else a lot else they are, though the drugs may also become their death and their foreknowledge of it, their depths.

In the summer of '78 Steve comes to Needles, California, and the house where my mother and grandmother live, with me and Ted and Anselm and Edmund. My grandmother infuriates me by suggesting I feed Steve: "Libby that man looks hungry. Why

don't you make him a hamburger?" One day we all go to the
river to swim; it's 110 degrees out and Steve stands under a tree
afraid of sunburn, fiercely unsmiling, making my sister-in-law
Kathy giggle quietly. He and Ted think the name Needles Point
Pharmacy is hilarious: people involved in drugs can be incred-
ibly simpleminded. We all, all except Grandma—Kathy and Al
and kids, and us and Steve and kids, plus my mother drive off to
L.A. in it must have been two cars, to deliver Steve up finally to
divorcing Effie and to go ourselves to Disneyland. We play the
new Willie Nelson, Steve's, all the way to Barstow; Willie singing
"Blue Skies" is an unexpected blast of poignancy and a song I always associate with Steve. Steve leaves us at the motel near Disneyland; we all get sick like dominoes, catching a 14-hour flu.
Exactly a year later, I visit Needles alone with my sons and have
one of the most upsetting dreams of my life, simply that both
Ted and Steve leave me: they walk down New York's 8th Street
to a bus stop between 5th and 6th Avenues, it's cold and the
sun's gone down behind evening's purple clouds and I know
they're leaving me for good. I wake up emotionally broken and
am under the spell of the dream almost all day; what I'm feeling, I find out in the future, is grief:

> There is precious little
> between bites
> but it is hard to lightly bite
> loved ones
> for thinking of dead ones
>
> That man's joy, that woman's joy
> comes to us
> not so much in similar words
> —quote or coincidence—
> but I think in lethal duet
> vowel train, crossword puzzle whim
> —a flick of the scat-capable wig
>
> The man I am thinking of
> is—good God—hereabouts
>
> and this is the Last Call he heard
> from the day he was born—O Ted!
> —"Drysdale and Mantle, Whitey Ford
> and to You," from *20 Poems*

Skipping ahead again. So much must have happened between '78 and '83. Marion and Steve's wedding at City Hall; and then the wedding party, attended by throngs, at 7th Street. She and I make and drink too much rum punch; Allen Ginsberg and Peter Orlovsky wash the dishes; someone probably Brodey stays forever, was it? Marion becomes pregnant and so they go to England to have the baby cheaply and properly; Marion and Steve move to Harris's apartment on 2nd Avenue near 3rd Street, way way up (Marion and Joe are still there now) on the top floor; Marion gets tired of being poor and sort of takes over Facts on File (she's still there too); Marion and Steve buy a huge TV and a big chair to watch it from, and dishes, matching. Steve teaches a little, Steve gives a few readings, but really Steve Steves: he takes care of Joe, gently, from in front of the TV, scribbles poems, freaks out, makes phone calls. "Alice, you don't give very good phone, do you?" Other works surface and sometimes disappear because they aren't deemed good enough: the legendary "Some L.A. Apartments," a poem composed of hilarious exchanges between people imagined to live in apartment houses photographed by Ed Ruscha. In a speech balloon the word "Bitchin." That's all I remember, though I used to have the tape of Steve reading it at Snug Harbor in the late Michael Scholnick's summer reading series, but I think I gave it to Marion after Steve died. Now, in the present, I discover I no longer have a copy of *Gentle Subsidy*—one of the loveliest of titles. I've lent it to someone. And I open *The California Papers* and discover sophisticated paragraphs that are I think about how to live being in some sense abnormal:

> Linens at which I glance for the hysteria of my senses. I had to know the apology to be recognized. Blank space next door to the present, dancing about the good. "Fine, pleasing." —Almost identical face. I see too much so abruptly while the other sings. To qualify my lingering: "A lovely night."

Let's see, a lot happens, of little things, and then Ted dies. Steve later tells me Ted came over shortly before he died and they lay on the bed together discussing "it." Or that it was in the air, Ted's death's upcoming. I don't remember any other particulars. Inside black shock waves we go on. So, there are poems to be written about that too (see above). And my sons need men to talk to, Steve being one. When Anselm, urged on by friends doing same, hops on back of truck which leaves downtown Eastside and doesn't stop until all the way through Holland Tunnel at which point he meets the cops and is taken back to junior high (late) and so I'm supposed to punish him: I make one of the conditions of his expiation be that he tell Steve all about it. That's because I know Steve in his hypersensitivity will be horrified, but also exquisitely gentle. Steve later informs me he was honored to be so used. Anselm hangs out with Steve on Super Bowl Sundays; Eddie visits Steve a lot, sort of out of the blue each time. Well Steve becomes more and more someone you must go to, I suppose there are intimations of things wrong inside him, physical signals he's picking up, he doesn't look so healthy. But he gives good phone; he becomes addicted to *Saturday Night Live* and Billy Crystal's Fernando Lamas imitation, he calls everyone up and says You—Look—Mahvelous! Peggy starts to hate it, probably because they phone each other almost every day and he won't not say it. You—Look—Mahvelous! One time, it's my birthday and Steve and I go to a show of early (pretty bad) Pollocks and then on to what's become known as Steve's Bar, a baseball bar on First Avenue where one has Buffalo wings and lots of beers. He feeds me a pill; we toast my forty-somethingth birthday; I wobble home. He and Marion seem in fact quite happy, even when they both look terrible, he in a sagging phase or she thin and drawn from pushing herself too hard; they are a "true" couple, a marriage of large spirits:

*Life in a Northern Town*

Six in the morning, outside
Blowing snow in the perfect dark, 22°
I'm awake after awakening dreams
(Often happens just before dawn)
Marion and Joe abed asleep
Joe wearing his earphones, radio going
I put them on, pour a glass of juice
Get some coffee going
Come out here in skivvies to write this
Loving them both so in a northern town
—from *20 Poems*

Of course, I don't like to conjure up the time of Steve's death, in 1989. In New York everyone seems to die in the summer. Every summer, for three years running, someone dear to me dies; and Ted too died in July. In 1989 I'm with Doug, have married the British poet Douglas Oliver (in February 1988). We've been at the Naropa Institute teaching poetry for a week, it's July, we've just come back. Tom calls from California to say Steve's had a heart attack and has gone into a hospital but he doesn't know which one. Doug begins calling hospitals and we discover he's been admitted to Beekman; we find Marion there; Steve, as I remember it, subsequently *seems* to be okay . . . Spends a few weeks in the hospital. I visit him there one day with a big sunflower. "Oh Alice, something from the natural world!" he says. We put the sunflower in a metal pitcher. "I watched *The Searchers* yesterday," he says, "it just came on that TV in the afternoon; I saw my father go off to die again and it made me feel awful." Steve gets out of the hospital in early August; I see him once before he goes with Marion and Joe to Silver Lake, New Jersey for a reunion with Marion's family; dies the night of his arrival. He has called me the day before the departure and said, "I'm afraid to go; I'm afraid I'll die." I've told him he won't. I haven't thought he would, although I'd been afraid he might in the spring; no matter your expectations, someone's death always surprises, it's never at the moment you might think of it but some other, horrible one. All year Steve has been working on a long national poem, scribbling on yellow legal-sized pads: only he knows how the pages fit together. So far and to this day no one else knows. "I'm writing about everything, about the whole country, everything."

It's the summer before that of his death that I publish *20 Poems* under the Unimproved Editions Press name. One of the twenty is now rather famously "Goodbye Forever," a page and a half long, virtually a list of expressions for goodbye:

> Shit, I'm busting out of this mill!
> Yes, I am! Getting out of this burg!
> Leaving! Quitting this place! Splitting!
> Making my beat! Making tracks! Hauling out!
> Heading out! Hauling ass! Heading elsewhere!
> Vacating the premises! Bent on all points other!
> Vamoose. . . .

Another, and both whatever they say have been written also for the pleasure of the words themselves, is the following "Song":

> The world will curl up
> The world will curl your remarkable lip
> And you will live forever if, quip well, abiding time
> Abides
> And seizing time flies to seasons of will
> and want.
>
>            Lended phonic semblance
> Rents promotion of the flesh.
> It is widespread lesser bucks
> Swipes delight,
>                and general flight
> Hobbles noted passage rites.
> It is massively same and seeming brief
> But gasp-lastly right.
>            It is a song
> Of sorts of usual and triumphant nature.

I write, in this essay, of the relation of poetry and life, the poet's life: they go together and echo each other, sometimes one has depth when the other hasn't (and vice versa). Steve (to continue in the present tense) lays his life on the line for and in his poetry, in order to write it properly. You have to give it something, everything actually, and I don't know what the it is in that clause, which it is, poetry or life. Poetry isn't a career, it's much more exacting than that part of it. Poets are routinely and shamefully used by their society to get a culture, to have a culture at all; Steve is clearly a culture-maker and the product of society's use of him. Abuse of his sensitivity. He has been hurt in his youth and the result is rampant poetry and also fear and instability; the more hurt you are, the more poetic you are, the less likely you'll be conformist enough, or have enough professional stamina, to get the circumscribed recognition a "famous" poet gets. That's the cliché, the cliché is true. If poetry isn't, as the theory people say, or shouldn't be about manufacturing a product, then poets such as Steve are the ones who should be given more attention. They aren't, and not by the theorists. You can't study him if you can't easily get his books (products); if he doesn't hang with a crowd of self-advertisers (theorists) telling you what his works mean and that he's the only one; if his life is embarrassing or something, if it works according to its own (painful) rules. If you can't separate the product from the producer, the poetry from the life. I love Steve so I'm not impartial or detached or whatever that word; I don't want to be that word; I don't want to be a scientist about poetry—and I'm not just talking about my friend, I'm talking about poetry. It isn't detachable. It's mixed in with everything, even when it isn't obviously being written; it's consuming and if you're a poet and you aren't somewhat ravaged from that, there's probably something wrong with your poetry. There's nothing wrong with Steve's, nor his life.

Steve is an Anglophile, and when he gets depressed he reads P. G. Wodehouse. He also loves the essays of S. J. Perelman, the *New Yorker* scribe. He doesn't seem to have a favorite poet, but he has constructed a mythology around a Dr. Sheldon Leonard who provides medical information on daytime TV. Steve, a hypochondriac, thinks Dr. Leonard a very good person. When he and Ted and Eileen and I compile (well it's a poem) our list of "non-sexists" Dr. Sheldon Leonard's name appears. Steve often hyperventilates and occasionally shows up in our living room with a small brown paper bag in his hand (to breathe in). Steve once performs at the Poetry Project, running a temperature of 102, reading haltingly, from a notebook, a long poem listing all the references to vomit he'd recently discovered on TV and in newspapers and books. Some people think this a disaster, I find it so on the edge as to be fascinating (still). In 1979 I interview Steve about things he likes, for a poem I'm writing: he likes the "manmade sunset," late-summer smog sunset; his favorite color is the red of curved Spanish roof tiles; his favorite flowers are Iceland poppies; the most delicate thing he's ever seen is the thin white line on a tire that's no longer made.

—Paris, December 1997

# Topics

*How could I assume a sound?*

# American Poetic Music
# at the Moment

I'm under the impression there was a rather urgent confrontation of the issue of measure in American poetry earlier in the
century, which climaxed in the documents of the forties and fifties (e.g., the essays of Olson and Williams) and subsided in the
sixties. It seems to me further that discussion of poetic music in
general has abated among poets, although the subject of "form"
or "forms" or "new forms" is often addressed. And there is a
sense that some poets are influenced by popular music such as
rap—well only rap; I haven't heard an American poet evince an
unexpected musical influence in years, certainly not to the extent of speaking of it. American poets tend to relate to measure or music now, to find and sustain it, at a level somewhere
below articulation of practice even to themselves. Poetry since
the fifties and sixties can feel like a game of subsequence: second and third generations, a time of "coming after." It's possible
that in the sound of our poetries we are utilizing the discoveries
of our forebears and might simply thank them for their gifts and
get on with saying whatever the people who come after have to
say. It isn't as simple as that, at least for me. I see my own poetic
career as a struggle—still going on, absolutely—to find a measure or sound that suits me. I need the discussion of this struggle for my own practice and meanwhile the sound of much contemporary poetry worries me. In a bad mood I think everything
sounds like prose—which is certainly worse than being prose—
from poetry in the *New Yorker* to bad Language Poetry. Or that
everything sounds like chanting or yelling. Or that, simply,
everything rushes on saying itself fulfilling itself, just in time for
the next poem to begin, the next same-looking same-sounding
mass of words.

The longer I write poetry the more I feel that I don't come
*after* anything. I belong to an initiating generation of strong

women poets for example. Not many people like me—if any—had published poetry before: how could I assume a sound? I never have, the problem has never been solved for me. Prosody is a real subject, how you or your thought becomes articulate in a precise time that won't ever go away. Prosody's a decision you keep having to make. I want first in this essay to discuss my own history in relation to musical practice, because it's out of myself that I understand the specifics of the subject as it refers to my generation. After that I will look at the work of some others, in search of the dynamic felicities I most admire. I will, throughout, probably be thinking less of the sounds of letters of the alphabet (though I may mention those) than of the rhythmical patterns established by syllables and words and lines.

When I was a very young poet I was consciously searching for a sound, what was called a "line." I didn't understand how people could be so certain of theirs: how you knew you wanted to use a particular line, how you knew it suited you. But I was never tempted to write predominantly in prose, or prose-like units, as a way out of my dilemma. Poetry is primarily the line; a poem tends to think by making quick sound associations forced upon it by the exigency of an approaching white margin. It thinks with music and thinks better—faster, more deeply, with more possibility of unexpectedness—than a work in prose does. When Edwin Denby says something as simple as:

> New York dark in August, seaward
> Creeping breeze, building to building

he lets the scale of vowels—*o-a-u-e-i*—erect a city in a seabreeze, delineating separate buildings, as he refers incidentally to Faulkner and de Kooning. In prose that would entail a longer process, creating space for a more intrusive tone of voice, creating an open-endedness perhaps; "building" and "seaward" wouldn't be interlocked like existential opposites which can't stay away from each other. All this because of an eight-syllable line, no articles, what a squeeze! Why would anyone want to give up such possibilities?

I, for one, wanted the line, with the white space around. (What's the point of all that white space? someone once wrote to me in 1973. It defines, I thought, as well as being a non-narcissistic possibility) . . . And so I worked at the line in various ways.

First there was the usual apprenticeship period of imitation: I imitated many men, exclusively men consciously, most successfully for me Denby, O'Hara, and Whalen. I was also taking from Mayer and Waldman what you might call the sound of myself— our generation of women making itself up and passing that sound around—but that was less deliberate. I learned a great deal about individual words and the spaces around them from Edwin Denby, but his line was too short for me. Although I didn't talk very much at the time, I suspected I was wordy. But who wants just to sound like someone else, even Whalen or O'Hara. How could a girl have a line? The very idea of it seemed owned by men. The assurance of it. How did they choose one, was the choice arbitrary, or signaled in a dream vision, how could they settle for one, how can you define yourself in that way, how can you keep to the mold, do you have a real name? The whole thing is arbitrary, given the metabolic and regional proclivities of a person of a certain character; but arbitrary in the sense that you do choose. And so I was always nervous, though defiant: my righthand margin has been called "nervous" and "eccentric" by various men and it is. For years I made my line be the width of whatever notebook I wrote in. Or wrote in conversational sentences like lines which I kept as taut as possible. Or even wrote in prose sentences, which I kept as taut as possible, as rhythmic as possible, so that they were in effect lines. Sometimes writing a poem I didn't have any problems, but in all those cases I was being imitative, either of traditional forms or of a form or style associated with a particular modern poet. Imitation is not a bad thing; tradition is not a bad thing. It certainly would seem good if it can help you bring off a poem more easily. It's just that I knew I wasn't that, that male-ish tradition as I'd been given it; and I did and do want to find my real voice (sorry, Ron Padgett poem "Voice") and my real self (sorry, Postmodernism) and make them in some way coincident with my poem.

By not writing in a rigidly conceived line, I learned a lot about keeping my so-called line alive, infusing it with all the vocal tricks I could think of. My work at best was charged with the rush and play, forwards and backwards and pirouette, of the speaking voice, trying to keep an invisible audience's attention in a moment-by-moment way. I didn't lay out lines, I dealt in smaller musical instances, which somehow materialized as uneven lines:

It's very interesting how I am
the ship & my sea is and yet
I must be seriously things, songs, & forlorn
little arounds sometimes. . . .

                         —"September's Book"

        At night the states
        whistle. Anyone can live. I
        can. I am not doing any-
            thing doing this. I
        discover I love as I figure. . . .

                         —"At Night the States"

In the first example I'm pleased with the way "forlorn" pulls its line out and then skirts around the corner and pushes "arounds" into high-pitched stress. In the second it's that everything slows and saddens by being in short sentences that are contrapuntal to the lines themselves. The line is divided into parts by the movement of the sentences—more about that to come.

Meanwhile—as I've indicated—the great dialogues on measure, ideas of the variable foot, projective verse, measure as tight pants in the New York School, had ceased. No live person seemed to be talking about the line anymore. When the dead were discussed people often acted either as if they'd said the last word on the subject or on the other hand had been crazy or pompous. Now Williams was never either of those things in relation to poetry. The variable foot is a brilliant viable conception and in practice doesn't have to mean those step-down triadic entities. It means what the phrase suggests, an American foot that is variable, possibly framed for scrutiny, a show of practice. It can make prosody visible, naked: at which point you'd better have some. What had gotten lost, I realized in the eighties when I wanted to write a long continuous poem, was the idea of the foot, or the idea of a smaller-than-the-line sound division. A consciousness that within the line is where the action is, the energy of the poem and the character or presence of the poet, as well as whatever connects her/him to the whole culture, the formal frame. That is, a line is not an arrow, it's its events. But contemporary metrics is all done by ear, on a level of intuition, thus it's achieved—a metrics or sound—through a process of imitation. In every part of poetry, in every school or division or style, a poet gets a line or practice, as I did, by imitating other people, other sounds. Poets used to do that too, of course, but not to the extent that we do now, because they also had the poetic foot to imitate, various feet in various relations, a shining grid. What I suspect is that if you're imitating a "poet" not a measure or a particularizable music, your own music becomes less precisely or minutely articulated, broadens or blurs. You go for a sound in general, hope you can bring it off; you perceive it in the arc or winding or blunt straightness of the whole line.

Well I'm not about to espouse a return to "foot"-consciousness; though if you wanted to write a long continuous poem, you would do well to think in terms of a foot. Williams, in "Asphodel" most especially, was onto a line that would be long enough to go on at length with but could still be slowed down and controlled, a long poem requires that pacing. But a smaller controlling unit doesn't have to—as the variable foot doesn't—contain only one stress; the pieces of a line don't have to be rigidly alike in any way. What they have to do is fit together. And interest the ear. A line is somehow "about" its divisions, unless a line is very short so that it is a foot—Creeley, Schuyler, Myles come to mind. But take Eileen Myles's stanza from "Basic August":

> If you saw
> my heart hanging
> out like the
> devil face
> grinning and pumping
> away sweating
> bloody and grimacing
> going ow ow
> ow! Kind of
> a furless
> pussy, my heart

It's most easily said all at once as a sentence rather than line by line. These lines are feet that pace you as you rush, rather than make you linger, and it's possible that the real "line" is the stanza.

I became involved in a new kind of foot/line geography when I created my line for *The Descent of Alette* in the late eighties. Here are most of two stanzas from Book I:

"A mother" "& child" "were both on fire, continuously"
"The fire" "was contained in them" "sealed them off
from others" "But you could see the flame" "halo
of short flame all about the" "conjoined bodies, who

sat" "they sat apart" "on a seat for two" "at end of car" "The
ghost" "of the father" "sat in flames" "beside them"
"paler flames" "sat straight ahead" "looking
straight ahead, not" "moving. . . ."

I wanted to write an epic, specifically a "female" epic, a narrative poem with a woman as a hero or principal actor, that had its own sound. It's well-known that there can't be a narrative epic without a generative line—a line that pushes towards more of itself so the poet can forget about it and tell a story. If the line is too long and quickly rushing, the story is over before beginning; if the line is too short the reader can't detach enough from it, lose consciousness of it enough, to be in the story. What I evolved for my poem was a line composed of phrases or feet, but I wasn't thinking of Williams, and I didn't think foot at the time, I thought "these things—units—I've discovered, which seem both to pace me and to make interesting configurations on the page." Each foot or phrase is its own sound event, but merges flowingly into the next, making a line: when I read from the poem aloud, I can emphasize either the space between phrases or the long total line. Either way I'm involved in more marked vocal accentuation than in my more usual more casual line: that's the effect of the quotation marks, which divide the phrases more emphatically than space would by itself as they tell the reader how to read the poem (another interpretation of the quotation marks might be that they are the instruction to the reader, Say this now, or Now this is said.)

The foot is highly variable, containing one or more stresses, and punchy and exaggerated, rather than discursive as Williams's is, though there are rather discursive sections, and also songs: the measure is flexible. There's a ghost of traditional English metrical patterning hovering behind my divisions, as there is behind most contemporary American poetry. We poets know we probably shouldn't locate it and fix on it rather than on the changes American speech has brought to bear on it. But I like having it there in the poem's rich subconscious. What I also hear now in this measure is a sound that comes literally from music, something out of popular or folk ballads. I think I was unknowingly influenced by Dylan's "Man in the Long Black Coat"; but as well I think I was probably influenced by Leslie Scalapino's short phrases in *way* and by the idea or memory of John Giorno's echoing repetitions. Those are two examples of a practice that involves a sort of infraline bracketing, especially if you take Giorno's stanzas to be his line and not the short lines themselves. However, most essentially my measure evolved out of two previous works of mine, the sequence *Beginning With a Stain* and the poem "White Phosphorus," in which I'd begun to use phrases in quote marks, but in order to create a chorale-like effect. Those earlier phrases are different, more sinuous or dactylic, being influenced by Monteverdi and Homer. The genesis of a sound is complex.

I've taken several more steps since *Alette,* worked on sounds/lines which can probably be seen as logical extensions of my *Alette* discoveries. In a poem called "Red Zinnias" I seem to join together something like the *Alette* phrases creating what I think of as a sort of harpsichord effect:

Crimson from the kermes insect
To see this color justifies being alive We all know that A friend of
mine knows a painter, blind from birth, who knows this
How does she see the crimson color? With a sense for that that guides her
painting hand Her works are very
brightly colored very bold

In this poem what one might think of as its units can be very much longer than those of *Alette* or short and abrupt. Some of the lengthier phrases are like harpsichord runs which can't keep from getting faster and faster. In another work, a book-length entity called *Close to me & Closer . . . (The Language of Heaven)*, which is partly in prose, the prose stumbles in phrases separated by ellipses in a very slowed-down version of the *Alette* unit. It's in the voice of my father who, being dead in an after-life, tries to explain what that's like and necessarily stumbles:

I have to . . . talk to you. I have to tell you . . . some
things I know now, I mean now that . . . I'm dead. See I see

this . . . <u>world deal</u>, where you are, clear—or clearer . . . I
see what . . . It's like, I see, a world where . . . it's going to,
not blow, but just . . . It's already, a <u>machine</u>. I <u>sold</u> parts—
it's all <u>auto</u> parts . . . gaskets & fan belts . . . batteries . . . &
gas. It's like <u>that</u> . . .

In addition to the use of phrases separated by ellipses, there is
the imposition of underlining here; I've laid over the prose a
web of stresses which tend to be counter to prosodical expectations. I'm noting the emphases of an extremely individual
speaker: I remember my father's speech as being idiosyncratic
as to stress, perhaps because his mind was moving faster than his
tongue. So in the third sentence above he's already way past the
significance of the word "blow" and ready to concentrate on the
word "machine," and in the next sentence when he emphasizes
the word "sold" and not "parts," he means "and real machines—
not the earth as machine—have parts and one kind of machine
is an automobile and I sold auto parts in my life and therefore
I know a little bit about machines and this present world as a
machine." He's thinking elliptically, like a poet, though he's the-
oretically speaking in prose; but his stresses, these stresses, are
what, for me, make his speech be poetry.

Since *Close to Me* I've written two books (*Désamère* and *Momma
and Red Hands*) which concentrate more on "line," a particular
line, than on infraline phrasing, and at present I'm simply writing again by ear, not at all striving towards a uniform line length
or particular kind of line. I suppose I'm hoping for an integra-
tion of everything I've learned in these books into a more automatically achieved vivid and various line.

I'd now like to look at some lines I like by other poets, selected on the basis of sustaining musical interest within the line,
of keeping one amused musically on a phrase-to-phrase basis.
The point will be to locate division, variation, play within the
line, and to further investigate it. For there are infinite ways to
stop and play, not just to segment and articulate a line, but to
be in it and enjoy the space, as if that were the whole point.
Here are lines encompassing a single sentence from "Red Shift,"
by Ted Berrigan. I will include the fragments of other sentences
that frame our sentence, in order better to show how the line
divides:

& Bowery in 1961. Not that pretty girl, nineteen, who
   was going to have to go, careening into middle-age so,
To burn, & to burn more fiercely than even she could imagine
   so to go. Not that painter who from very first meeting. . . .

The overflow of sentence to end midline, and the frequent com-
mas, are a characteristically Berriganesque method of breaking
up a long line into units which are somewhat linelike themselves,
here reinforced by the simple internal rhyme, twice, of "so" and
"go." But not, never, consistently; Ted would never create a pattern of consistence. "Nineteen" and "To burn" are short phrases
which break up a potentially familiar lyrical sound—almost nineteenth century—into something more spoken. The unit which
begins "to burn more fiercely" is wonderfully long, like a string
being pulled out. Ted worked very hard at these effects, was obsessed by this kind of metrical or musical closework. The result
in this period of his writing (late seventies and early eighties) is
a group of very singular considerable poems, characterized not
by ongoingness—everything pointing next, as in the poem-parts
of *Alette*, which of course tells a story—but by the poem's pointing back at itself. Taking the reader back into its intricacies. It is
monolith not continuousness.
   Here now are three lines by Joanne Kyger from *The Wonderful Focus of You:*

*July 20*

You left
   your heart behind, over there, back there
Sleepy slow Buddha, you catch up to me, OK?

This is really two lines, isn't it? But "You left" is given a begin-
ning-of-line emphasis, which means that the quickness of "OK?"
balances it by being a split-second tack-on phrase not spelled
out or even punctuated with periods. What's in between is in
phrases of somewhat various length; they aren't exactly linelike
or footlike, but each does pull its own weight, partly by being
unexpected in content, partly by being slightly different in
sound. "Over there, back there" is a surprise after "your heart
behind," it's casual, playful, almost pidgin-like, after the possible
Tony Bennett cliché ("I left my heart / in San Fran-cisco").

"Sleepy slow Buddha" is as slow as it should be, countered by the quicker "you catch up to me, OK?" Joanne is always doing tone-of-voice tricks, more interested in the whole moment when something good gets said than in the push to make more. Her poems emphasize the importance of individual words or smaller utterances and require the reader's willingness to stop for a moment and let something seemingly little become important as it's infused with reality, with poet's and reader's total realization of what's going on. Other people trying to be casual produce more lines; Joanne defines a shape already in progress—flick-of-the-wrist stuff. Her poetry makes me think of raw white voice squiggles.

The following is from "Historiography," by Lorenzo Thomas:

> . . . In the memories
> And warmth of their bodies where our Bird
> Stays chilly and gone. Every cat caught with
>
> A white girl wailed Bird Lives!

I notice that as I choose rather randomly these examples, I never light on a line by itself or even two; I'm selecting a lot of wrap-around sentences instead. As I noted earlier, line and sentence are both "lines" in a lot of contemporary poetry, set off against each other. The line is often broken into smaller, interesting sections this way. In this example, from "In the memories" to "chilly and gone," we have really a sound from Poe's "Annabel Lee" ("the wind came out of the cloud chilling / And killing my Annabel Lee"), but repunctuated, because the lines are broken in an un-Poe-like way, into a counterpoint to that sound. Then after that lush, anapestic sentence, suddenly the monosyllabic, funny, hard-to-say (but not so hard because of the line break after "with"), "Every cat caught . . . !" There's such amusement and enjoyment emanating from the author in these two sentences— there's so much sound around in the world to play with, really.

The previous examples by Berrigan, Kyger, and Thomas were all written in the seventies; I tend to associate this sort of poetic music or dynamic, which stays and plays, with the sixties and seventies. Contemporary poets born before, oh, the late forties are/were still conscious of the idea of a metrical foot and dealing with its loss. Open-field poetry, of which Berrigan and Kyger are both frequent practitioners, often deals with the articulation of phraselike or footlike shapes, helping the reader to speak the poem exactly, in the face of the disappearance of formalized guiding rules. Most open-field poetry seemed to have disappeared by the eighties, which were—along with the nineties— characterized by longer poems and by lines and structures designed to help the poet state or support difficult ideas; deliver messages, sermons, exhortations, etc., or shape a performance; or keep a state of fragmentation in suspension. The latter tendency has curiously enough resulted in a sameness of sound within works, because there has to be a sameness of something: sound, I think, has gotten designated philosophically most disposable. As for performance poetry, performance doesn't depend on nuance-on-the-page, but nuance-in-performance: rigidity on the page can be more helpful to the performer, in the way a score is rigid. And with the articulation of difficult ideas, of stories, of lengthy scenes, the point is to keep going until it's stated—the poet feels the urgency of not forgetting what to say, not running out of steam. Another factor in the nineties of course is the computer, which encourages wordiness and onrush and thus sameness, high speed rather than nuance.

Here are some lines by Simon Ortiz, from a poem called *Two Coyote Ones,* the decade of whose composition I don't know:

> this
> blonde girl came along. I mean that.
> She just came along, driving a truck,
> and she brought a cake.

I like the passage a lot, though it's much more placid, less jazzy or intricate, than the previous examples. Let me narrow it down to two lines "blonde girl came along. I mean that. / She just came along, driving a truck." I'm becoming quite enchanted by those; they move calmly monosyllabically slowly, they don't push to their ends somehow, they sit, they take up space, exactly; they take their time. I suppose that's what they do "within themselves," in the terms of my quasi-argument. Ortiz reads very slowly, and with his voice in my mind I'm aware that almost every word, even syllable, is potentially a stress and thus a foot. "I mean that" feels sonically brilliant, not shiny but inspired, but it's so plain. It pushes in, gently, an overlap, a layer or reminder of the one telling the story—from a past—into the present of the telling. Ortiz is from Acoma Pueblo and is much involved with traditional storytelling; a pace that comes out of his background is a transformative agent in his line.

Here are several unconnected lines by Fanny Howe from her sequence *The Quietist,* published in 1992:

> Doves leading—each white and practical.
>
> All the black around them gay
>
> "Advance to the fire and play with it."
>
> Sex is made on a bed which is too loose

At first I wonder why I've chosen them in this context. They're striking, somewhat traditional—they have a life on their own in that traditional way. Which way, looking at them, seems like a good thing; one stays gladly in each as if it were a room. However three of these lines end quite oddly—all end oddly as to meaning—but three "sound funny": "practical" is a quick blurty syllable cluster; "play with it" and "is too loose" are strangely flat, conversational, again clustery. *The Quietist* is a sequence in which visionary or mystical experience is being described as exactly and compactly as possible, though that's most explicit in several prose passages: "Consequently, I experienced a self-presence which can only occur when the upper soul has departed. . . . I had died before my own eyes!" Each part of the field of this telling, become each line of poetry, is somewhat strange. You're not meant to take the lines quickly at all and are pushed back into them by the way in which they end. The exigencies of a specific problem—how to present a "mystic occasion"—have resulted, in places, in a line which walks towards a tradition and then pulls away from it slightly, almost as if in order to stay alive. As if a manifestation of the problem of how to be a religious mystic *now.* It's the play between what's traditional and what isn't that makes these lines lively within themselves.

Here is a passage by Paul Beatty from "No Tag Backs," in *Joker, Joker, Deuce:*

and spellbound en tre pre neur'i al black capitalists
silkscreen malcolm x on crew neck t shirts
for nubian humans

He's telling you exactly how to say it, slowing you down and making that a joke, exploiting open-field a bit—making you say it the way that he hears it. The task of the foot or the line is to make the reader enunciate and stress as the poet intends. An urban African American, Beatty wants to make sure you say his line like one. Like both Ortiz and Howe he shapes the line to suit his experience of life and language and sound.

These examples—and the previous ones as well—point at a shaping of the line or foot out of individual needs, in a different-each-time way. Evolving needs caused by the inclusion in the national poetry of people who previously might not have been thought to be there: women, African Americans, Native Americans, but also people with a working-class background. With the latter reference, suddenly my selection of examples makes sense in another way. The lines by Ted Berrigan—who came from a working-class background—take on a different coloration considered in this context: for you do hear it, his working-classness, for example in the use of the very ordinary word "go" in the midst of old-fashioned ornateness and echoes rather than a conscientiously hip sound—this is not top-university-smart poetry, it's making itself up out of the known past of literature and the real present of ordinary people. It's in this context that my own poetry seems less eccentric than motivated by the urgency of making sound accurate to previously unpoeticized aspects of life. This is not just the same old multicultural stuff, it's to say that the line must change for us but syllable-by-syllable all over, because we're each whole. And yet what we're making isn't unrecognizable. But something makes the poem or line or phrase happen properly, some instantaneous magical unity of voice, world, word: it should happen *all along* the line. I'm not here in life to phase anything out, not here to be just half in this experience. I read poems, other people's poems, silently by articulating each word mentally; the poem exists in my body. The poet places her/his sounds quite literally in me. I therefore want two things of the poet. One is a sort of constraint—I don't want to be violated or incited, no one has that right. The other is, I want to be amused. I'm capable of quite intricate dances, because my life—anyone's life—isn't simple. Metrics is in the real feet too, dancing on the ground I mean, all that, the Greeks and the tabor, Africa, etc. I can understand intellectually that someone might want a non-metrics. In practice everyone has a metrics. The more the subject's considered by the poet, I think, or up to a point, the better the metrics will be. Really, I want to know what other poets think they're doing. And I'd like in general a plainer discussion of poetics which depends on, as metrics does, a constant renewal as the occasion of speaking is renewed, a new definition each time, no jargon or rigid vocabulary.

It's obvious to me that in the treatment I'm offering, much if not most of what makes poetry musical remains unstated. There are conventional ways of dividing poetic music into parts: rhythm, pitch, selection of consonants and vowels, the interplay of these elements, the establishment of patterns: "free verse" seems partly to be held together by intonation patterns, the repetition of sound forms (see Douglas Oliver's book *Poetry and Narrative in Performance*). I've concentrated mostly on rhythm so far because it's what I'm most conscious of in my own writing. I feel, however, as if I should pay some attention to the other elements, to pitch, melody, tonal shift: but I never think of those as such, what I think of is "voice," "my voice," "her or his voice." The voice is the instrument of poetry; though it becomes ghostly, generalized, when a poem is read silently on the page, it's still sensed, as if there were a way to hear a voice intellectually and not in the ears. For example when I read the following delicate lines by Leslie Scalapino from a bizarre sexual description in *Defoe*—

> Some people slip ahead on the ground.
>
> they're on their knees. slip ahead.
> this is after.

—I don't hear her voice, which I know and which is a particularly distinctive one; I hear, probably, a version of my own voice, but a mental voice with no timbre at all and only a little in the way of pitch. A voice isn't just its scientifically analyzable components, and that's especially so in a poem. Now a great deal of what I hear in the Scalapino lines is rhythmical, or metrical, something done by the phrase "slip ahead" and its repetition, and by the use of two long lines and a short line together. I also hear the liquidity of the lines, they slide (slip) out of the mouth/mind without stoppage except for the periods, an effect of choice of consonants. But I hear voice; I hear the fact of a person speaking, I hear tone-of-voice; most especially I hear the passage of the lines as a voice, the words stick together in my silently reading mind as vocal continuum. A poet's talent is of the voice, it's what she organizes and dynamizes—not words by themselves but this essentially bodily production by which the poem is played and replayed in time. Thus a poem has a great deal to do with the individual who composes it, though it doesn't necessarily have to remind us of that person in an up-front way. But the total musical or sonic effect of a poem is individual, of an individual. A reader projects her own voice, to some extent, into the poem she's reading; but something unfamiliar in the poem will keep her from making it her own. In the beginning of trying to read Leslie's lines I can hardly say the line "this is after," because I would never say it in my life. I might say "this happens afterwards" or "this comes later," which have more stresses and are less delicate. I know I wouldn't think of writing "slip ahead," which I'm quite interested in as a phrase. It plays, in my mind, on "slip away" and then "steal away" and then "look away," which have connotations for me from songs. But Leslie is describing specific physical action, not following after verbal echoes; she's also describing her own voice. Of course I'm talking about word choices, but what makes you choose is very mysterious and has to do at least partly with a sense of what sounds right in your own mouth. Is that statement irreducible now? Maybe. At any rate it brings me back to the beginning of my essay: what is my sound?

A poetry career is in some sense an exploration of what sounds right in one's own mouth. The question, for me, is never settled: as everything changes so quickly, there's more to be said about this world, and change seems to require different ways of saying. I've been variously, over the years, formal, experimental, elliptical, polysyllabic, exceedingly plain, personal, and narrative; also speedy and slowed-down; all, it seems to me, in the same general voice. Perhaps you can't say of my poetry "You can always tell who it is," but once you know you can see it. Something makes the poem, whichever poem, sound like me. At this point do I know what it is? I have mannerisms, am aware of them and do exploit them: choose kinds of words repeatedly in characteristic formations. I have preoccupations of sound and subject, which can change; access, as I've indicated, to various lines or metrics and vocabularies. I presumably have a personality, in the high-school sense, or a character, in the traditional-novel sense: neither of which I, frankly, care much about, except sometimes to keep a dinner party going, but that aspect of me can have to do with my voice. Etc. etc., but none of that's it; a voice, a poetic voice, is a unity, a one thing that despite new coloration, socialization, change, has an absolutely individual distinction. But I myself can only—not be it, because I'm not my poetic voice, rather I myself can only write it. I have some control over many of its characteristics, its accomplishments, its range, its disguises; but it always finally eludes my control, because in the fact that it is, and in time, it's autonomous. It doesn't consist of parts and characteristics—and so the familiar circumstance that no poem is ever what one intended or pictured. And one can't reproduce another poet's line, be like the poet one imitates. In fact, one can't find a line, still can't find a line. I still don't know what my sound is. You identify me, I don't exactly.

Joanne Kyger has said, "Time is a nice thing to go through." As one goes through time one acquires a certain definition, a shape in terms of society; a person, because of certain choices and circumstances, seems to become *X*. But is always what unfolds in time, something that can unfold, which is more definite and more mysterious than its trappings. That's the voice. As a poet, I learn how to put it in lines, in sentences, in "feet," in the guise of many voices; but it remains essential and essentially unstale, panicking slightly at the next step it takes, above all itself. It could die, in the going-forward sense: I could stop writing and that seems fearful. Have I stepped away from the topic of music? No, music's an organization of sound in time, life in time. I think we all (poets) should keep talking about that.

# Voice

Poetry is vocal. So far. Forms of poetry that aren't vocal—concrete poetry or textual poetry that's difficult to read aloud—seem slightly other than it; a voice carries poetry. I can almost imagine a poetry of telepathy: a transference of thought in which the density and simultaneity of thought are also transferred, obviating linearity and therefore voice. But time implies a voice, and though there might exist a sort of "page" meant to be taken in all at once and not linearly, the page would most probably have been constructed linearly, letter by letter, and that linear construction is the author's voice. An author's voice is existence and presentation in time. And it's existence that is her and is later of her: it comes, came, directly from her body. Writing's a string of what can be read aloud; and poetry is still rhythmic speech, or should I say spokenness. Usually, these days, but not always, written down; a transference of language from the author's own physical being. Who best reads a poem aloud? As all poets know, it's usually the author. What is an author? I'm one; I made the poem be the way it is. What relation does my poetry have to me besides the fact that physically I make it and thus know best how to say it? That's complicated. I would say that the voice of my poems is not my daily voice, my voice "in life"; it's mine by virtue of issuing from me, but it doesn't present me so much as it does my poems. My voice connects the letters and words on paper; they won't exist without it even after I'm dead. It will always be me that makes the poem work; it's embedded in or with the fluid of my voice.

Since a voice is usually produced by a single body (and in much of collaborative work the goal is to produce a single-sounding voice), it is bound up automatically with such attrib-

From *Raddle Moon* 18.

utes as presence, authorial presence, personality, and unity. There is in Western poetry no decentered self, perhaps unfortunately; but I have read no work produced in Western society that doesn't reflect, among other things, the personality, experience, motivation, and ambition of the person who wrote it, except possibly for some very bad work by third-rate or pseudo practitioners. In traditional societies works exist which are somehow a single voice of that society, constituting a communal poetry produced over centuries of societal definition and of artistic manipulation, simplification, and change. It's true that any individual Western poet's work expresses both a tradition of form and thought and also contemporary speech, practice, and opinion—reflects many others, other voices, you might say. But a poem nevertheless is of a person, one person, not society.

There is no way not to impose yourself as an author on your material. In the late seventies and early eighties I wrote a number of poems containing many voices. I used peoples' voices verbatim, from the room and also from the street and from the media; I thought at the time I was being practical about writing in a crowded apartment, though also I was in a state of fascination with the voices of others. I thought as well I probably didn't have so much to say on my own, in terms of "saying something"; but I knew I had things to make and wonderful materials. Now it seems clear to me that I invariably created a unified work, out of various peoples' voices and words, which reflected my individual self and situation. Consider the following passage from the poem "My Bodyguard":

> They have those tiny pepsis at the corner store.
> They're thirty cents now.
> Ask a wino for a nickel.
> I'm just making sure I don't have to go to the bathroom.
> Put it in positive subsidy.
> My wife never got 500,000 dollars from the Iranian
>     government.
> I just want to do the same old thing differently. But I feel
>     too slow and a little blind,
> like Ellen Terry in her blue glasses.
> I'll take the garbage down.
> It's all smeared.

I'm Rainey Hughes of the Dallas Cowboys.
This year I had some problems with the wind.

This sequence of lines is fairly disjunctive; certainly people are speaking, one doesn't know who. Yet the passage has an overall feeling that's a combination of humorous and sad. There's a sense of a "problem" or problems: financial, physical. Or perhaps a feeling of dead end. At the time I was only writing down what I was drawn to—I didn't have time to think because speech disappears so quickly as it's said. But an author's choices always reflect an author, and in every kind of poetry there are choices to be made, even in poetry dependent upon chance operations.

I'm trying to remember if, when I was writing poems such as "My Bodyguard," I was attempting not to have a unified voice. I don't think so. Nor was I trying not to infuse my work with my presence, though I was definitely not interested in "the personal" at that time. I thought I was not of much interest, and possibly somewhat voiceless, but I didn't have a theory about it. I wrote whatever came up next. Yet the seventies and eighties were apparently a time of people wondering about voices and personal selves; in all sorts of places and ways recently people have been ambivalent about voices, about whether each one has one or wants one: as I've indicated I've come to think one's stuck with one, by virtue of the existence of the single vocal apparatus, brain and writing hand in the single body, which tends to speak, I'm afraid, uniquely. Here is a poem by Ron Padgett called "Voice":

> I have always laughed
> when someone spoke of a young writer
> "finding his voice." I took it
> literally: had he lost his voice?
> Had he thrown it and had it
> not returned? Or perhaps they
> were referring to his newspaper
> *The Village Voice*? He's trying
> to find his *Voice*.
>                What isn't
> funny is that so many young writers
> seem to have found this notion

credible: they set off in search
of their voice, as if it were
a single thing, a treasure
difficult to find but worth
the effort. I never thought
such a thing existed. Until
recently. Now I know it does.
I hope I never find mine. I
wish to remain a phony the rest of my life.

It may be, as Padgett seems to imply, pretentious and misleading for young poets to search for a unique and wonderful literary voice. However, judging by this poem, Padgett has found his own. This poem exemplifies the dominant voice of his work after the sixties: forthright, casual, jokey, but also serious. There are things he does with this voice in other poems that are surreal, descriptive, abrupt, or tonally modified; but this is the voice, Padgett's voice. One can see from this example that such a voice, that speaks so directly and easily, might even as it changed tone or subject or even, almost, style, still point back to Padgett's mouth. It is exceedingly flexible.

Here is a very different kind of voice. These are three consecutive stanzas from Barrett Watten's long poem "Progress," which consists of similarly constructed stanzas:

Now a large-scale construction
    Being built.
            In Siberia,
    Belief dismantles machines
Covering 1/6 of the earth. . . .

Say Chiang Kai-Shek,
                think of
    A Fabergé egg in principle.
    But is it a song containing
Error that is 100% poetic. . . .

I am making things difficult
    For myself,
                to spread out
    And advertize this camera
In place of orbs of the eyes. . . .

This stanza form houses a voice which is ingeniously allowed to start and stop and bend around line ends but never to go on too long in any one trajectory. It's as if the poet is trying both to act against and exploit the voice, which might be characterized as educated, thoughtful, lyrical, anti-lyrical, ironic, serious, media-imbued, etc. Its characteristics might be argued about, but it has characteristics. But the voice is more than those characteristics, it's the fluidity, the essence really of the poem—what makes one read and unfold with the poem in time. The successful attempt to keep the voice in check punctuates and heightens the voice's attraction.

At the moment, the voices of women poets of previous generations are fascinating to me again. Their voices seem to come sharply into focus as urgent, particular, unified, and trenchant. If one isn't allowed a sense of one's importance in the world, if one can't participate fully in the literary and political struggles of one's times, perhaps one's voice becomes not diffuse or secretive but even more pointed and characteristic than a man's, who must always sound a little like the other men he has discourse with, both the live and the dead great. Here's a portion of a poem by Emily Dickinson:

> I love thee—then How well is that?
> As well as Jesus?
> Prove it me
> That He—loved Men—
> As I—love thee—

What is this voice like, well direct, ironic, passionate, and above all audacious. In the first line of the quotation, it divides into two, asker and answerer, creating movement and play. The parallel phrases in the last two lines are pleasurably bitten off, one can hear a voice doing it. There's nothing in the way of the voice in this poem, for example a sense of what a poem *ought* to be saying or, even more, the kind of poem a person or poet like herself says. She just says it—the poem—and it's shocking, especially knowing that she and everyone around her believed in Jesus. Of course "she" doesn't say "it," a voice was once released from one Emily Dickinson to articulate on paper these words. Why can't I imagine a man writing this poem or one like it? Partly because it's blasphemous without tact or argument or romance of blasphemy, because no one's listening. And it isn't conventional, a woman writing for no one wouldn't have to observe convention. Convention serves men well since they've usually invented it: this is not a cheap shot but factual observation. Literary discussion is still a male enterprise in most poetic circles, and the male poetries of the twentieth century are still permeated with the discussion and in a sense its conventions. Think of Eliot, Stevens, Pound, the Williams of *Paterson*, Olson etc; plus whatever one's chosen contemporary movement: who's doing most of the theorizing? Probably men. And don't their poems support even explicate their theories? This is the perpetual creation of convention in poetry, though I'm not at all implying that convention is bad necessarily, but it can be rather imposing. A voice is all that can cut through it.

As we all know both literature and the male world at large have complained a great deal about women's voices. Since in poetry women's voices don't sound the same as men's, we are told our voices are quirky, nervous, or guarded, dry, or "too" something: flat, strident, emotional. Stein's is too coy, H. D.'s is too quaint, Moore's is pedantic, or Gwendolyn Brooks's school-marmish. Kyger's isn't ambitious enough, Myles's is too self-centered, Scalapino's is both opaque and odd, etc., etc. All of which makes me think more that poetry's essence and flow is voice; and that women with their "flawed" and blatant, in whatever way, voices, will carry American poetry into its next stage. American poetry needs live voice, not anti-voice, and not a dead literary voice. I'm disappointed that some contemporary women poets might want to give up "voice," as if that were possible or good. Voicelessness wouldn't make a point that anyone outside a coterie would get; veiling the speaker hedges issues and responsibility for what's said and what's lived, individually and communally.

Gertrude Stein, who may certainly be called one of the ones who invented this century's poetry, did so with a voice, one that's well-known for its ability to irritate as well as attract and stimulate. I myself go through alternate periods of liking it excessively and being rather irritated by it. Here is a passage from "More Grammar for a Sentence":

Supposing three things a will they be having met and at a time with while and after without not at a time with which to trouble with advising why they weeded without grass. Because they prefer separating salad. This and they come alternately again. It cannot be naturally a paragraph because they are there and they have left one shovel so they will be willing which is why two hundred salads are as small and will be larger. A paragraph is an hour.

After every day they think.

About their wheat which is coated with bread. And they like grapes. Because a dog looks at it as a ball. Why if they are currants and made it with it.

If a dog looks like it does with them.

It is very nearly a paragraph to cry.

There is nothing in Stein but—I'm tempted to say—voice; hardly ever anything but. What is this voice doing here, it's explaining the nature of paragraphs and sentences by making them. What is it like? A combination of intellectual and domestic; playful; capable of being suddenly and deeply probing in a way that feels both inhuman and poignant. The arc and flotation of Stein's sentences are exactly her voice. *The Autobiography of Alice B. Toklas* demonstrates this, the voice in its long buoyant sentences, which are the inside-out version of the sentences of her "difficult" works, is Stein's and Stein's only. Alice B. Toklas in *What Is Remembered* speaks rather tersely; Stein's sentences are a letting out of a shining ribbon of voice. Stein on recordings reads with absolutely no tone of voice. She is presenting you with a voice so whole that it is an abstraction, or ideal, without nuance. What irritates people about her voice is its insistence on its choice of mannerisms, which seem like idiosyncrasies in the face of more standard expression—how men have said one must say. It's not so much that she's hard to understand as that she seems to be having her own way far too much. And rubbing it in. I'm using her here, therefore, as both an example of a woman's voice and an indication that any voice flows from a self and does "self" things, as well as going about the selfless business of the poem. The poet "enjoys herself" and "forgets herself."

It must be even clearer by now that a poet's poem voice is not at all the same as a poet's person voice. The voice of the poem isn't interested in the poet at all. The voice of the poem is interested in the articulation and outcome of the group of words it's generating: that is to say, it seems to have come into existence just a moment prior to the poem, and though it doesn't exactly cease with it since it reverberates so, is really only for the poem. Take the Dickinson poem already quoted from. We recognize Emily Dickinson's poetic voice seemingly from other poems, but that voice, or the voice as that, isn't what counts while reading this poem, we're in the one situation of a lone block of words while we're reading it. "I" has just begun to exist for us, I is not Emily Dickinson or Dickinson's poetic voice, I is I in the poem's situation and doesn't spread further without the reader's doing extra thinking, extra work, in repeated reading. The reader feels inside a particular and small construction of language which spreads out in concentric circles creating eternities around it and between it and her other poems. Obviously one would not make a speech like this in conversation. The poem's too carefully constructed, too rhythmic and sonorous. It may be making a point that Dickinson wanted to make to or in relation to a specific person, but in conversation practically no one would say I love you more than Jesus loves the world. No one would want to either. The things that are said in poems are for poems—for the unity of the occasion of a poem, which is made by one poet only. In life one person blends with another, but rarely in poetry. As for the Dickinson poetic-voice part, this is and isn't the same voice which says "I heard a fly buzz when I died." The same directness and intensity are there, but the two occasions are utterly cleft from each other, each is a cosmos; a poem is usually more important than its voice.

A reader may wonder if a poet who uses the first-person singular and speaks apparently of her own life knows exactly where life ends and art begins, where the real voice and the art voice separate. I think certainly yes. Take the following very short, untitled poem by myself:

> Clouds, big ones oh it's
> blowing up wild outside.
> Be something for me
> this time. Change me,
> wind. Change me, rain.

A specific feeling and occasion prompted it, and it still embodies something I can feel; but I wrote it hoping it would be as if spoken by anyone—hoping anyone could "use" it. That is, I know it sounds like me, but while being read it might live inside anyone, being some voice of theirs almost, through sympathy and imagination. But when I wrote it there was a real storm outside. I was in art and life at the same time, as I hoped my reader might be, but somewhat differently. When I wrote while people were in the room, as with the earlier passage from "My Bodyguard," and conversed with others as I wrote and wrote down things I myself said, I was also conscious of the border between art and life: I seemed to inhabit the two simultaneously but they were very distinct from each other, like two stories of a house.

In most cases one writes while alone or comparatively alone and—and this is perhaps the most important difference between the person voice and the poet voice—in most cases one is not speaking. An internal voice speaks, and for many poets it is as if the poem were being spoken *to* them as they write it. Furthermore the voice of the poem doesn't seem to come from the brain, i.e., the part of the person that willfully imposes preintentioned meanings or constructions. I've asked various poets where in or around the body the poem voice comes from for them and for example Anne Waldman said the voice comes from deep in the chest, Allen Ginsberg said that for him it is the throat and that he actually feels his vocal chords vibrate while he writes. I myself used to hear the voice come from just outside my forehead on the right side; now I'm not sure, different places, something in the mouth or maybe from the eyes. This phenomenon underscores for me the physical, vocal nature of poetry and the unitive nature of it. I think the poet's voice takes on a life of its own, but that it's from the poet; it's as if it has to get free of the pieces, the mess, of the real person and regroup as a unity. Then suddenly the poet is there not the person, not thinking anything but the poem being written, in her voice and in her style.

What is it that makes someone's voice or poetry so different from another's? That is in a sense to ask a question about style, but it's more than that since styles are shared by groups. I think on the other hand anyone is confident they can tell X from Y (members of Z group), though anyone might say to put X or Y down that they sound like everyone else in Z group. The truth is that voices are distinctive—both poetic voices and personal voices: no two people make very similar kinds of choices as to words or references or sentence or line evolution or sound patterns or metrics. And certainly not all of those together. It isn't just because people *try* to sound different from each other. Actually poets are often trying to imitate some master or model and failing and sounding mostly like themselves. In a living poet's poetic voice, there is often the awkwardness of not sounding like what one is imitating that was declared great in the past, there is also the excitement of that happening, that which makes the poet different. Specifically there are say the places where Great Poet X might have made a characteristic run but living poet Y can only manage the kinds of things Y says. Ted Berrigan said "feminine marvelous and tough" in imitation of Frank O'Hara, but O'Hara would not pile up adjectives like that, he would do some fast dance in between them; people are very happy with Berrigan's line. Voices are quite different from each other. Comic impersonations can only go so far: a president's vocal sound and the style of his speeches may be imitated in terms of a few aspects that are stylized and static. In real life, anyone's real life, something more fluid is always happening, the world is always changing, nothing can be predicted, including a voice or especially a voice because it's always reacting to different circumstances. In poetry one has the ability to revise what one has written, but one can't revise the world one is reacting to; a poet can invent a world in a poem, but that is utter novelty, requiring presumably an even more unpredicted voice.

It seems to me that there are at least two important qualities that a poetic voice should have. The first is fearlessness or courage, the voice must be clear about itself in some way, believe itself, and be consistently unafraid. We are speaking now of a voice not a person. And I might add further things, that the voice shouldn't be afraid of being wrong or getting caught up in awkwardness or messy intricacy, or changing tone or emotion or diction, but mainly the voice should speak fearlessly, assuming its authority is equal to any other voice's—as far as speaking itself is concerned. The second quality that a good poetic voice must have is difficult to characterize, it's something like vividness, actual presence of the live poet in the dead words on the page—the poem is very little without that, and very few, comparatively, poems have that. To make that transference is a mysterious thing to do and no one who can do it can teach the skill to another person. Neither of these two qualities implies aggression, righteousness, or usurpation of place: they simply imply being.

# Thinking and Poetry

I want to discuss how to think honestly in connection with how to write honestly. I want to oppose these two "how's" to thinking and writing in accordance with received ideas: those that come to you from others, the outside; or your own old ideas, what you think you think and don't question anymore. For it's very difficult to be honest inside yourself; you tend to slide over tough places hurrying, saying, "Of course X is the truth, A, B, and C thinkers took care of that for me," or "At this point everybody knows . . . ," or "I know what I think about that, that's settled." If that's how the mind behaves how can there ever be a new poem? I'm convinced that as in reasoning, in writing both poetry and prose there must be a progression in which each unit is clearly rendered (what "clearly" means I'll deal with presently) and words are clear as they occur. There must be something to hold onto so it might be assessed and even disapproved of by the reader. If a poem primarily creates a world to inhabit, that world should have well-defined contours, or if the contours tend to dissolve the dissolution process should be clear and shapely.

My wish for honest thinking sounds so . . . clichéd. It's what I've always wanted of my own writing/thinking self and used to assume everyone else wanted and practiced to the extent that they could. I believed that poets must be engaged in a struggle with the truth, or truth as the present reality of this world: how to say this world. I believed this could only be done by being as ruthlessly honest as possible, within myself, and in the poem perhaps more gently, but certainly syllable by syllable, without jargon, jargon being words coined by specialists in other fields, which represented privileged knowledge, had little color, and were transitory. I thought we all wanted to think and speak for ourselves; I didn't think we should be in agreement. But now I believe that the world is full of subscription to the thought of others, and that originality and quality of thought and expression do not win and worse will not necessarily win in the future, which used to be the "real time" of the best poetry being written presently. The world, both the big orthodox world and the small avant-gardeish world, desires conformity of thought and style. And whatever mechanism preserved much of the best for use in the future is breaking down under the pressure of the existence of so much stuff, text, "thought," "communication"; whatever is different or presently unappreciated may be smothered. Who will find it? Who at this point "knows" anything, reading so much? I see a world of literary and poetic hacks, become that under increasing careerist and businesslike pressure to "sound right." We shouldn't all use the same kinds of words in our poems and our thinking, shouldn't produce quite so much, we should be puzzling a little more over each conclusion or line that we write. But the buzz of the dialogues already in process, the terms and styles, are so seductive it's tempting to replicate: everybody will like you and what else counts but a group of like-"minded" people, what else does reality consist of except such a group and its enemies?

It should be the poet's business to test, *continuously,* current assumptions, rather than assume them. I find being a poet something that must start again all the time; I'm always reinventing my practice, discovering what I believe is true and how to express it. I haven't changed much since I first began writing: I never understand what to do or how to do it, I understand that I must start and will now by an awkward process make something, thinking hard and deeply about each part as I go along, sometimes quite fast though—you can think accurately writing rapidly. I remember quite well when I began writing. I took a prose-fiction course as an undergraduate and was assigned to write two stories, having deliberately placed myself in the position of being forced to write. "Write a story." How does one write? Unit by unit, I thought, that's the only way I'll get it done. Word by word, sentence by sentence, also, in terms of the story itself, action by action. I visualized my stories exactly, a set of actions taking place within a short stretch of time, consecutively, hardly any breaks. I modified this method in various ways in successive stories. I discovered "telling" as opposed to presentation of action—telescoping the action into narrative; longer time frames which allowed the characters a life outside that of the particular story I was telling; flashback, etc. Then after a couple of years I discovered the stream-of-consciousness and automatism. A loosening up, a change of style, so that there was still a story unfolding which I was in control of, but written in a language which another part of me controlled, a more unconscious part. I think with these two methods I established the basis of my subsequent practice in poetry: an attempt at a balance between conscious and automatic controls, with the conscious part more careful, for honesty's and clarity's sake, and the unconscious or automatic at the very least available for a deeper veracity's sake. This process, this balancing act, seems both how one makes and how one thinks. A story is paradigmatic of how we think. We make story-shapes in our mind out of our own experience, out of both everyday happenstance and unexpected fantasy and projection of possibility. We have predictable thoughts and unpredictable scary thoughts. We think about something "rationally" but then we become "paranoid." Or even "dishonest," projecting on others guilty responsibility or full bad character. It's possible to indulge in sloppy thinking both in life and in art, in a story for example to plot an easy next action not a truthful one.

But why do I say that one, in writing a story, keeps the conscious-control part careful "for honesty's and clarity's sake"? Why should a story or a poem or a thought process have to be honest, and what is clarity? Honest here means true. Would my character "Tony" (as I remember it, having kept no copies of these stories written thirty years ago), a nice small-town high-school student, really get himself into a situation where he winds up seriously injuring someone with a broken beer bottle to the face, at an abandoned house in the desert? This was my first story, and I was troubled over this question; I was so undecided that I can't remember now if in the story someone else did it but Tony was certainly implicated, or if it was an accident by his hand that was precipitated by a violent atmosphere, or if he did it under group pressure. I used, and still with trepidation, very simple language, because that way I could see the action best, following it brick by brick. I didn't want to hide anything, not even about myself and my skills, or I wouldn't learn anything about literary structure. I wanted to make it clear to everyone I was a beginner. (The humility I possessed then seems unimaginable to me now.) Also I think I knew even then that it was essential not to fudge the story with respect to truthfulness because the issue involved was so important: to what extent is a normal and good person susceptible to violence or participation in violent situations? The movies suggest that violence comes easy, and much of fiction does too. I've never, however, believed for a minute that Meursault killed the Algerian in Camus's *L'Etranger.* In my story I named the main character for a friend of mine and visualized him as that character so I would be careful about what happened. The real Tony, a person for whom I've always felt affection and respect, wound up being blown up in Vietnam about four years later. He was the nicest person imaginable; he participated in a very violent situation, as we all did by extension, and he died. My story was therefore important and relevant not trivial, and it had been important to be honest and clear.

How is a poem like my story, are the two comparable? When you write a poem, you sound it, test it, unit by unit, for something like rightness, which includes truth, no matter how "obscure" the poem may be to others, and for clarity, at least of form or dynamic if not of obvious meaning. Here is an early poem of mine, but written quite a bit later than the story I've referred to and certainly after I came to understand something about the unconscious part of writing:

*Dear Dark Continent*

Dear Dark Continent:

The quickening of
the palpable coffin
fear so then the frantic
doing of everything experience is thought of

but I've ostensibly chosen
my, a, *family*
so early! so early! (as is done always
as it would seem always) I'm a two
now three irrevocably
I'm wife I'm mother I'm
myself and him and I'm myself and him and him

But isn't it only I in the real
whole long universe? Alone to be
in the whole long universe?

But I and this he (and he) makes ghosts of
I and all the hes there would be, won't be

because by now I am he, we are I, I am we.

We're not the completion of myself.

Not the completion of myself, but myself!
through the whole long universe.

This is obviously a monologic speech of someone involved in a reasoning process. The steps and parts of it are clearly steps and parts and they can be, as such, agreed with or rejected successively. It's possible to disagree in an overall way with a poem as being wrongheaded or phony in tone or situation, and certainly a poem works in ways that aren't linear. However the linear procedure of the poem should be either true—evident, unblurred—or disputable in terms of what it says or how it says it: that is, clear. It's possible to be unclear by merely asserting a style or a language, with the belief that one must be saying or doing or making *something*. The poem "Dear Dark Continent" is clear; but I myself have problems at times with parts of it, and why shouldn't I, I've changed since I was twenty-six years old. I remember writing it, and how releasing it was to say "palpable coffin" and the funny lines "fear so then the frantic / doing of everything experience is thought of," and to ride the pronouns. However I don't always know what I meant by "quickening," which is the word for when the baby starts to move during a pregnancy and which I had recently learned. I probably meant I was that much closer to death by having had a baby, the "palpable coffin" is the body, which quickens in relation to death in this instance rather than birth. These lines are not completely clear because I can forget for a time what they mean, but they are clear in the sense that they are a knot—they aren't a blur. A knot can be untied. I have the most trouble with the conclusion: are "they" "myself"? I'm not sure that they are anymore. I'm not so sure that others are in any lasting (not in the world's eyes, but in the universe, the whole long universe) sense oneself. How honestly did I believe those last lines when I wrote them? They say that my son and husband are myself, though not the completion of myself, because I'm not yet completed, but myself because my life is myself. I think I was pondering at the time Frank O'Hara's emphasis on a sentence from Dr. Zhivago: "You in others, this is your soul." I had, in a certain way, bought it; but I don't buy it anymore. I don't at all think "you in others" is your soul. But that was a good thing to believe then because I needed to be taken out of myself, I needed emphasis on my life in others. I bought the sentence as truth: I found it hard to think O'Hara could be wrong about anything because he wrote so well. No one should ever have an attitude like that towards any writer or figure whatsoever. No one. Don't buy it.

Then what am I buying right now? This is the question everyone should be asking all the time, What am I buying, in terms of thoughts and ideas, from others? What are the parts of my reasoning I'm not sure of, but tell myself I am? Am I thinking at all, or am I producing masses of "style" containing a few "hits," just creating a sort of verbal environment? Or letting whatever language comes out of me do its work . . . new things said, meanings, a wash of, oh, created life. As I myself became a more sophisticated stylist, the temptation simply to verbalize, to make something or show off, became stronger. A lot of the time I just wrote stuff, still do. Sometimes that's how I open the door to the next phase of my writing. I used to think it was all publishable as a record of mind or consciousness; I don't think so now, am not interested in work that doesn't have a clear rational shape as well as the pleasure and truth that come from more mysterious depths. I don't want to become the automatic part of me, I want the automatic part of me to become me. That is, I trust my conscious self. I don't like the world outside my door very much but the best of myself is awake and clear. The "I" I most prefer sits serenely and somewhat numinously behind my personality, behind a sort of window, watching the chaotic and distressing events of the world. I can't often act as that one but it's the one I most really am. The automatic or unconscious is a gas, as we used to say, and may know a lot too; but a lot of it is stuff that has to be organized.

At the moment (late 1994) I'm in the process of writing poems [they became the book *Mysteries of Small Houses*] which are more deliberately honest. My project is to describe the nature of the self, using my self as a model. Obviously honesty is called for, not "language." I'm disallowing any preconceptions (to the extent that I can), existent terminology, previously thought-out attitudes, and most bias. There is the bias of my life itself, what I think because my life shows I think it. The only cliché I'm using is the word "self," so people will know what I'm talking about. How successful am I, how does this process feel? Telling the truth has a unique feeling about it. Truth-telling doesn't come in a wave of self-assertion but loftily and neutrally, or coldly, or sadly, sometimes warmly, but never self-righteously. In these present poems I'm happiest with what I'm saying when the metrics themselves are "truest," that is not worked at but also unexpected: I don't know the truth in advance, the words for it or sound of it. I know it somewhere in some way or I wouldn't be able to discover parts of it, but the truth can be kept alive only with new and honest words. If I find myself writing for a succession of days out of a self-righteous feeling, out of a showing-off-for-a-specific-audience (either entertaining or haranguing them) feeling, if I'm straining too much towards a metric that's herky-jerky or automatic (too old), then I know I have to make a change in mood or procedure.

There are houses in the mind with front doors that never get opened, that have on them the signs of one's supposedly basic beliefs: "soul is you in others," "unified self," "white men are evil," "the truth is daily life," "reality is language," "no god," "god," "my business is to help others in obvious and direct ways . . ." One rarely unlocks the door and enters, dusts off the shelves, forgets what the neighbors think long enough to find out what it's like to live there. I have a preconception in the book I'm writing, that there is a unified self and that the pronoun "I" is a word which should be given back to people, who need it, but deepened. However I'm living in the house of that preconception as openly as I can, pointing at the furniture, occasionally breaking the knick-knacks and spilling espresso or Contrex on the rugs. I'm trying to say what I know and I'm finding that honesty is difficult, interesting, and unexpected. The more I write this book the more I discover about self-censorship, that it has more to do with fashion than anything else. One tends to tell a modish truth, to adopt the vocabularies of fashionable theories and disciplines (philosophical, literary, scientific, sociological, psychological . . .). There are truths one has sometimes told oneself but has never bothered with in a poem because no one else was writing that kind of poem and therefore they didn't sound like the kinds of things to be said in a poem. There are also things one thought one had said but hadn't, because one had said them in the vocabulary of the times and therefore left out much that its conventions didn't admit, or had said them in the vocabulary of a particular form which had its own conventions.

Here are the last eleven lines of a recent poem called "What Do I *Have* to Write?":

> Give the child the Protection of
> the President of the
> United States
> give her a vitamin a volume and a
> *nom de guerre*
> my name is Alice
> I go to school
> in Pleistocene Dream
> but having
> ruined me you have nothing
> further to teach me

They say things similar to what I've said in other poems. There is an implication of human impermanence and of vanity as indigenous to the species, with a reference to a recent and even specifically American ruinousness. But I made the point differently in the other poems because they were narratives, story-poems with characters speaking; I didn't state the case with regard to my living self because I didn't want to say "I." That's not a fault in those poems (*Désamère, The Descent of Alette*), which I think are very truthful. To say "I" in the above lines, to speak with this meaning in reference to myself, is to speak another, perhaps more pointed "truth": I personally have been ruined, any individual has been ruined by the civilizations we know. You don't have to agree with me, but please follow the argument. Current poetic convention doesn't allow one to say such a thing, not by being against saying it so much as by not thinking of it. If one subscribes to a school that is in favor of saying I, one might say, America you're trying to ruin me with your racism, classism, sexism; or in another of the schools, middle-class life is drably ruinous; or I may be ruining myself with alcohol, drugs, sex, and America is a contributing cause. The subtext in the first case is usually "but you won't," and in the second and third cases "I rather like it." In my lines I say flatly that what our civilization has taught me (and I mean me) has ruined me and I don't like it. I have spoken as plainly and as simply in previous phases of my poetry but I didn't say this sort of thing, I said some of the things one said in clear poems in those days. I said some other things too which were a surprise to me, but I would never have said anything so negative: our conventions at the time would not permit that, and I was young and optimistic or at least oblivious, and eager to become as happy as the poets who were slightly older than I seemed to be. How could I do that without imitating their tone and attitude? I did become happy, and I am "happy" but I am also "ruined" because it is human society's business to make me that way. So at the same time as I'm "happy" I'm also agonized over (a) the gulf between my daily and often trivial social self and my real self which I am only rarely; and (b) my participation, which I cannot seem to control, in the impoverishment of other people and especially in the sudden destruction of this planet's ecology as it's stood since the last ice age. I take this situation to be both international and personal, and I do mean that with regard to both (a) and (b), which in some ways seem exactly the same. Then these are the things, I reason, I must say in my poems; must not allow any convention of thought or style to keep me from saying. In the face of what must be said, does it ever matter if one says "I" or not, if one tells a story or not, if one uses certain forms or not? Say what must be said.

# Women and Poetry

What a poem is, how it is good—what it looks and sounds like overall, the kinds of subjects it's concerned with—all of this since when? since shortly after known history began, has, worldwide, been addressed by men with some input from women. A poem, looked at this way, is "male," most ways of composing and setting down lines of poetry, of grouping them into poems on the page, seem "male"—the choices to be made are largely from among male solutions to male-generated formal problems. In poetry, as in everything else, one hardly knows, rather, what is "human." To come suddenly back to this place this time: even the revolutionary generation of American women poets now in their forties or so are working from a position of modifying what men have thought and done; and the most supposedly radical feminists among them, in order to subvert the Western intellectual tradition, borrow from it to speak—who knows the difference between them and it? There are no forms of poetry that are entirely "owned" by women: what studies of women's poetry seem to show are predilections for shapes and subjects, what our poetry tends to be like. This is rarely to say that we have made something very new, though there have been *at least* two geniuses in the last two centuries, Dickinson and Stein, of the sort to conceive some radical formal departures—Dickinson still working within the given lyric, changing American metrics though—Stein's most radical works being both prosy and difficult, and those two qualities together making an inadequate answer to the question: What might be a true female poetry? (Prose really isn't the answer, isn't a poem, is too sonically narrow, too singled-planed.)

But the real question is, is that a real question? What might

From SCARLET, no. 5 (September 1991).

be another kind of poetry? Whole other poetry springing from nowhere, as at the beginning of the world, in the hands of women? Or perhaps even more desirably, as at the beginning of the world, invented equally by women and men together. Not, as now, already made out of men. Do you follow me? I'm saying, there may be *nothing* of women in the way *any* poem looks now, in what its *form* is—the entire soil, all layers and most nutrients, are for all practical purposes male. What would it be like to make a female poetry? Is that possible? A desirable way to conceive an undertaking? What would another poetry possibly be like? Can there ever be any value in sexual polarization of activity? Is there feminine and masculine? as well as what women and men each have done (I've not been talking so far about what men and women are like, each sex, but about what they've done—who owns the forms, who is quickly moving in on the, possibly, same forms)?

The question then perhaps becomes, What is it like at the beginning of the world? I mean hopefully now—but the world is late and ugly. But we pretend anyway that we are the first ones, we open our mouths for the first time (there never was such a time), we speak with the first voice ever (there never was such a voice)—what do we say? Why must we have a poetry? And who are we? We see now that we are the world and the world is poetry, that words are our poetry, while other pieces of the world have other poetries—birds have their songs but also plants have their forms and patternings and the sky has its own look and process: poetry is the surface and texture and play of being, including the light that springs up in things from their depths. Then what is a poem? The poems are everywhere, we walk among them—an infinitude of them occupying the same boundariless space—what are they? Our knowings of what is: born to know we are each being, born to be aware in the heart of being, we gently define shapes of being, in words, which are free of dimensions, free of cause and effect, free, but when they're completely free, formless, senseless, also useless and meaningless— why bother? Poems are part of our being alive, to realize them, to say them, is completely natural to being alive: to say what we've done, how we feel, what we know, in such a way that the poems we say are as much like the poems we walk among as possible. As full of foliage, thick air, and our own exquisite terrors, perceptions, enlightenments, as full of interpenetrations of mind as the world is—narrowed to the voice that comes out of the mouth of the poet. Only one person at a time says it, even if, as at the beginning of the world it is the myth made up by everyone. The responsibility is of one voice (for few people are poets), but are our voices similar? Are they more similar at the beginning of the world than they have become at this late age? Who then can be a keeper of the voice? Does that person have to be defined, among other things, as a man or a woman, or is that to do humanity, or one's tribe, a disservice? One supposes that she must only be "the voice," that is, ungendered.

Thus hopefully no one and anyvoice, a woman sits down to write now, 1991 by "our" system (we know what sex invented "our" system), to invoke the first voice, that first voice ever, to say a human poem of this world. But it will speak through the arm to the pen against the paper: she will not say it in air, around the fire, it won't return back to where it lives, in the air. It will exist on a two-dimensional surface that's in the shape of a rectangle (though it will still also exist in mind and performance: air). But it has been defined . . . so. And if she chooses to break a line in a certain way, if she chooses to write in prose sentences, if she chooses to leave much white space often between words and phrases . . . all of these are the male-made packages we know so well, where is the poem? The real poem sticks in the throat: to write in these ways is not the answer. Machines, tape recorders, video recorders are not the answer, that ruinous decadence; nor sound and movement on a stage—a stage is not on the level of the audience, movements upon it are exaggerated, it is not itself where any poems are. Where is the poem? Where can it be? The poem we can't find is a whole new earth, I think, how will it be made? Everything we do now is wrong, but we can't just stop doing—but as there is too much of garbage too many people, too much that's material, there are too many same thoughts, same actions and gestures. Too many written poems, multifarious and yet the same. Pilings up of more and more, to what end, when the world is like this? Women and poetry, wasn't that my subject? Finally we are allowed to write but the world is dying— the poems are dying—the literal ones I mean, at least seemingly. In this ridiculous inescapable and tawdry material world we women are allowed now what? To make more of it, more of that, more stuff. But not to remake it. Not to change it from the ground up and walk out onto the earth as if it were its first morning. Walk out and see being all around us, see the real poems. The sons-of-bitches in Washington and Wall Street and L.A. are still sons and rich ones—admitting a few exactly like-minded bitches—and worse, still self-perpetuatingly powerful in the tiny glassed-in bubble that contains all the master controls. Very few people, male or female, seem capable of making a life that doesn't conform to the patterns that so benefit these tyrants. Finally we are allowed to write, hysterically pile up pages in a dead-end world using dead-end forms of articulation written on dead trees. Everything must change and very very soon. Women and poetry, is a joke—Where is the world? Where is the first world? We must find it as soon as possible.

# The "Feminine" Epic

This talk will mostly concern my book-length poem *The Descent of Alette* and will be both personal and literary, unapologetically. Would Dante come to talk to you about *The Divine Comedy* and not refer to his banishment from Florence? Of course I don't mean that I'm like Dante; I mean that my poem comes out of what I know that's communal knowledge and that I've suffered privately. Like a soldier, like anyone touched by political madness. In the mid-eighties I'd begun to wonder if it was possible for me to write an epic, I mean I'd begun to wonder dispassionately about the form. But there was a crucial moment. My brother, who'd been a sniper in Vietnam, was beginning to be in emotional trouble; and one afternoon I stood in my apartment in New York and thought to myself, just exactly this clumsily, "What if my brother in Vietnam was like a Nazi, and I by extension am? And what if I therefore owe an epic?" I wasn't sure to whom I might owe the poem. That moment closed over and I didn't think about the connection between my brother and epic for a year or two more. It was the same time it took for me to arrive at a formulation of the difficulty of being a woman and wanting to write an epic.

I began to move towards the epic first out of a sense of the twentieth-century "Big Poem." I'd become interested in Olson again, mostly in terms of his geologic-mythological connection. The earth has a past, and present, formed in rupture by godlike forces. And his presentation of pieces, beauty of fragmentary past, and present, as reflected in the look and feel of *Maximus*. But I started to be intrigued by the possibility of telling a *continuous* story, not in the manner of Olson, Pound, Williams, but

Delivered as a talk at the New York State Writers Institute, SUNY Albany (October 1995).

more in the manner of Dante or Homer. Because it seemed so difficult; and I already knew how to negotiate pieces. So many people in this century seem to.

Meanwhile, and this is as important as any talk of technique and strategy and aesthetic, my brother began to enter a state of extreme crisis which I (we) came to understand too gradually and too late. He developed acute post-traumatic stress disorder, became heavily addicted to drugs, was admitted to a succession of hospitals which didn't seem to know how to treat him; finally entered a rehab and underwent a kind of cure. That is he kicked the drugs and found out a lot about himself, managed, in his mind, to give some of the guilt back to the national community, where it belonged, but still died, accidentally OD'd a week after leaving that rehab.

An earlier death as well was part of this process. Kate Berrigan, my stepdaughter, died in a traffic accident a year before my brother, and in her honor I made my first attempt at something epic in scale, since being devastated by her death, I felt close to large dangerous powers. I kept trying, in what turned out finally to be a not-that-long (thirty-some page) sequence, called *Beginning With a Stain,* to find a story for beginnings. The beginning of the universe, the beginning of living again after someone loved has died. But I didn't really have a story to tell, or a cast of characters, so I couldn't make an epic. Then, the year afterwards, as my brother began to move towards his death, I began work on a poem, "White Phosphorus," which became his elegy. At this point I began to grapple with the idea of a female or feminist epic—but not calling it that in my mind, rather, an epic by a woman or from a woman's vantage. Suddenly I, and more than myself, my sister-in-law and my mother, were being used, mangled, by the forces which produce epic, and we had no say in the matter, never had, and worse had no story ourselves. We hadn't acted. We hadn't gone to war. We certainly hadn't been "at court" (in the regal sense), weren't involved in governmental power structures, didn't have voices which participated in public political discussion. We got to suffer, but without a trajectory. We didn't even get to behave badly, or hurt anyone as a consequence (that would have been a story). I made my poem "White Phosphorus" be somewhat about this subject, and it like *Beginning With a Stain* had something epic about it, but it wasn't an Epic, though it had a partly Homeric sound. But I made a prosodic break-through writing it, developing further a measure or method I'd stumbled on while writing "Stain." The last two poems in "Stain" are written in a chorale-like way, in long lines divided into phrases set off by quotation marks. Here is an example:

"In that dark before a messenger was released" "&
do we return there?" "in that dark" "but, and dreams" "I
have never drea . . ." "in our dreams we catch up with the story, and
the darkens-back-to-the-first-dream, the fragrant" "it wasn't
fragrant," "in this dream of the first dark, I" "it wasn't dark"
"dark as water silk dark quiet no-limbs dark, no-skin dark, it's
so dark, but, not foreboding or heavy" "it isn't
dark"

These are singing, dialogic, quarreling voices. In "White Phosphorus" the voices are unified and the measure begins to regularize:

"Whose heart" "might be lost?" "Whose mask is this?" "Who has a mask
& a heart?" "Has your money" "been published, been shown?" "Who can &
can't breathe?" "Who went" "to Vietnam?" ("We know who died *there*")
"This was then" "Is now." "Whose heart?" "All our heart" "the national
heart" "Whose mask?" "has its own heart?" "A mother's" "mask"
"Whose money" "do we mean?" "A woman's money" "Woman's money". . .

It was the discovery of this measure that made writing *The Descent of Alette* possible—that and finding a way for a woman to act, to commit actions, enact a story, that suited the genre of epic. With regard to the measure part, I don't think you can write a real epic (as opposed to the twentieth-century Big Poem) without some, even a lot of, regularity of line. I wanted something regular, but also catchy—not some prosy long-line spinoff of the what-had-come-before; I'm afraid I wanted something all my own. As I worked on the first part of *Alette,* the line of the previous two poems evolved into something I could depend on, not think about, have to invent while I was inventing the story. I needed more freedom to tell the story than a constantly changing metrics would allow me. Thus I arrived at, and stuck with, a four-line stanza, each line of which consists usually of three to four feet or phrases:

"A man" "in a suit" "in the first car the" "front car of the train—"
"This older" "distinguished man" "asked me to" "ride with him"
"join him" "I declined &" "moved back" "far back, I" "joined a
car" "that contained" "women &" "girl children" "women in skirts"

"girls in dresses"

I've never analyzed the measure in its smallest parts, the actual
phrases. The measure itself has been called, in effect, feminine,
or at any rate a break with the male conventions of line and layout. I don't particularly think that that is the case. My line owes
something to other poets including both men and women:
William Carlos Williams certainly, H. D. probably, Leslie
Scalapino a little, John Giorno a little, Bob Dylan a little, others.
However I discovered that after I'd finished the poem. Furthermore while writing *Alette,* and now too, I thought of this measure as My Measure, that "My" not being sexed in my mind, even
though the poem is finally predominantly feminist. How could
a measure possibly have a sex?

The story part is different, its technique, for me, is sexed.
Well I *don't* act. I don't even believe in acting, at least not very
much. Why did I want to write about a woman of action if
women don't act and if I don't really approve of deeds? I do live
and some sort of action in time is entailed in living itself. And I
wanted, and still want, flatly, to write an epic—to take back some
of what the novel has stolen from poetry and, further, to avenge
my sex for having "greatness" stolen from it. This may be ambitious, and even self-aggrandizing, but also it may be necessary.
But actually I like stories, though not so much in novels; I like
them in poetry, where they're more compressed and elegant,
where the movement of the story is reinforced by the movement
of the lines. I wanted to tell myself one of those. I discovered
meanwhile the Sumerian epic *The Descent of Inanna.* In combination with my observations on dreams and on myth, this poem
pointed me in the right "story" direction.

May I summarize briefly the story of *The Descent of Inanna?*
Inanna, the queen of Heaven and Earth, puts on all her royal
trappings and symbols, and goes down to the Underworld, her
sister Erishkegal's domain. She tells her servant that the other
gods must be informed if she doesn't return soon. Why she goes
is not explained except insofar as the Underworld has attracted

her focus. When she arrives in the Underworld her sister orders that she be stripped of her clothes and her powers, presumably like any person at that door; her sister fixes the eye of death upon her and she is hung up naked, dead, on a meat hook. Soon her servant begins to visit the gods to plead for their aid, but only one god, Enki, doesn't think she's "gone too far this time." He makes two creatures from his fingernail dirt and sends them on down to the Underworld to help Inanna. Mysteriously, when they arrive, Erishkegal is in labor, naked—she's always naked—lying moaning on a bed. The creatures sympathize with her as she moans (she doesn't actually give birth, again as in a dream she's simply "in labor"), so she offers them a present, "the river" in fact. They ask instead for Inanna who is then magically brought back to life. But she has to find a substitute for herself, for her death: someone to take her place in the Underworld. She returns to the Upper World surrounded by the *galla*, demons from the Underworld who will make her choose a substitute, but everyone—her son, her servant, etc.—loves her, has mourned her, how can she banish one of these to the Underworld? Hah! her husband Dumuzi isn't in mourning, but happily sits on *her* throne; she fixes the eye of death upon him, as her sister had upon her. He runs, hides, pursued by the *galla*, changes form several times to escape them, is then betrayed by a friend who reveals his current hiding place. But he has a sister who hadn't betrayed him even when tortured by the *galla*, Geshtinanna the goddess of wine and poetry. When he's finally caught a deal is cut whereby he and Geshtinanna will take alternate six months in the Underworld. So it's then a pretty familiar working out of seasonal patterns.

*Inanna* is a long chanted poem presumed to accompany religious ritual. It contains symbolic action, mythological or dreamlike action, the kind of action women do participate in, at night in sleep, or deep in their psyches, when they tell themselves secret stories about their lives, when they tell themselves stories almost without knowing they are. *Inanna*'s story is linear but not natural and full of spaces; not all meanings are told or strings tied up. The main protagonist is a woman, the most significant other protagonists, except for Dumuzi, are also women. It isn't a "woman's poem" though, it's about forces—life, death, birth, rebirth—since those are what goddesses are, they're not people.

Inanna doesn't "act," she does nothing but show up in the Underworld, die, get revived, and choose a replacement. Compare that with the *Iliad*. I found I could use such a poem, though not very closely, as a model. My poem isn't really like *Inanna* except insofar as Alette descends into an underworld, and insofar as the action of my poem is mythological.

May I tell the story of my poem? The protagonist at the beginning has no name, no identity or memory. Finds herself in a vast subway system ruled by a well-educated, well-bred, multi-talented male Tyrant who lives aboveground. The protagonist wanders from subway car to subway car, station to station, observing the misery and minute particulars of the Tyrant's control. There are animals and also metamophoses in this system, and she begins to be aware of a connection to a snake and to an owl. She also begins to know she is on a quest to find "our mother," the First Woman, whoever that might be. Finally she gets on a different kind of train which dissolves and leaves her floating to a lower level of existence, a set of caverns representing the psyche. As she proceeds from cavern to cavern, in a way reminiscent of her progress through the subway system, she is presented with explanatory tableaux or dreams, which show piecemeal the structure of the self below its surface. She also picks up the trail of the First Woman, who may be a snake. At the end of these caves she participates in a sort of lottery, draws a card, the Ace of Panthers/Roses, which signifies that it is she who must kill the Tyrant. Then she descends a staircase to a further level of being, a natural but entirely dark setting, a potential paradise which contains no light from the sky. There she finds the First Woman, not really a snake though that has been her symbol—but headless: her head is always nearby. The First Woman tells her story, and the protagonist assists in the replacement of the First Woman's head; then the First Woman begins to place stars in the sky, simply by speaking. The protagonist leaves her and meets up with the owl, who performs on her a brutal ritual "death," in order to give her "grace" and the owl attributes of flight, a beak, and talons: weapons. Now ready for the Tyrant she ascends to his mansion, a huge literal Museum of Natural History. They tour the museum with its displays and dioramas. The Tyrant informs her he can't be killed because he literally is the world and not at all a person. They reenter the subway world together, take a train to the River Street stop, outside of which flows a dark river. The protagonist sees a black tattered cloth floating on its blood-black waters, and having swallowed the cloth she regains her memory and her name: she is Alette and is in mourning for her brother who died in one of the Tyrant's manipulative wars. There is a pursuit, a sort of combat, and she does kill the Tyrant, discovers the one way to do so, which involves use of her owl powers. Then the doors of the subway unlock, people emerge, and the world begins again in open air.

To highlight some of the feminine or feminist elements of the poem:

I deliberately reversed the Dantean, Christian, and other religious direction of "enlightenment," making it a descent into darkness. That is explicit in the poem as a defiance of male tradition. Enlightenment is seen as a male luxury.

One of the major story elements of the poem is the search for the First Woman. She, as I've said, turns out to live on the lowest level below the ground and to be headless. One of my poet friends accused me of making simply an Earth Mother. As if that were a bad (un-avant-garde) thing. But she isn't an Earth Mother, she has gone to live "below" rather than "above," to escape the degradation she'd experienced in the upper world. Her most marked quality is that she's a storyteller: though she has no operative mouth, being headless, she can speak from the throat, and she has the ability to make you *be in* her stories. Really then she's like the source of dreams. Perhaps I'm saying that the split between conscious and unconscious began with the almost universal banishment of women from public and political life. To make her a storyteller here is to suggest that dreams are stories and women are the world's veritable dream-masters.

Other fables throughout the poem relate directly to feminism. The poem is in fact saturated with such material, though the Tyrant's subjugation is more than a subjugation of women: it's a control of the forms of most people's lives, of everything except death and the more profound reaches of spirituality. I wrote this poem in the late eighties, in New York, when suddenly the homeless were everywhere. My personal problems—my brother's death and my powerlessness, even my lack of literary recognition—were part of the general problem. I thought I had discovered all by myself the concept of the Dead

White Male, the Tyrant being one of those who never dies. Because only *they* were talked about again in the eighties, as if the sixties and seventies had never happened. As if someone like myself would never count. When I first heard of DWM in the media, I knew my poem was true and my thinking was right. And public. As an epic traditionally is.

※

At a certain point the problem of the poem became, can one kill? No, one can't, but the Tyrant isn't alive, he's everything that isn't natural being. So Alette *can* kill him. I began the last book, in which he's killed, three times; I couldn't get him till I found out he wasn't a person so I didn't have to hate him. He's based physically on two men I like very much (I'll never tell their names). Some people really like him: "I was on the Tyrant's side myself," the writer Johnny Stanton said to me after a public reading of Book Four. It seems traditional to epic that the other side be attractive. In the *Iliad* which side is "ours"? In Milton . . . Satan. In Dante, Satan is a beast, but Hell itself makes the more popular poem. But I was "mad at" all the epic authors when I wrote *Alette:* they were my own fair enemy and they, too, were the Tyrant.

I didn't know I was still writing, so specifically, about my brother's death until midway through the last book. That's exactly the point where Alette remembers her name. My brother's name was Al, mine is Alice: "Alette" is more like "girl-owl." In another poem I call it "owl-appendage," as "-ette" appends. In a world of war like the one we live in, woman is appendage certainly, even if she joins the army. After I discovered that my brother was behind the poem, I went back and built him more into it. Though I was writing it because of him, all along, I'd forgotten, because the poem isn't personal, it's public. Though feminist it includes everyone. It's dedicated to my father, another Al, because he's the owl in Book Three. Alette's father has died and become "natural," an owl, and so is able to show her how to be powerful enough, from Nature, to overcome the Tyrant. You kill him with Nature, since he isn't natural. It's possible to kill Nature for a time in a small space—a planet even; but there's always the Universe, the larger Nature. It's a winner, certainly. It swallows this planet.

I've since written two smaller narrative books, one of which is perhaps epic-like; the other is more of a poetics or book of spirituality or both. I wrote the latter soon after *Alette*. It deals very little with the literary or life problem of being a woman. I had discovered a further problem: the nature of the "black lake." In *Alette* the third or lower level of being would be Paradise—ultimate unexclusive self-realization I guess, except for the Tyrant, because of whom it can *never* be Paradise. Women are outside of any named Paradise or Heaven or Nirvana, they are stuck in history waiting for it (history) to be righted. They have not participated in the dialogues of Paradise, they have not founded religions, they have not been represented at the inception of any meditative or spiritual tradition, they are "-ettes." Alette's father, the owl, like the First Woman, is as well only in the quasi-Paradise. He is unintellectual, he is natural, isn't religious even. However in the middle of the third level there is the black lake, the gate to the rest of the universe, death, infinity, the one place beyond the Tyrant's reach. I realized, after *Alette,* that I had to think about that lake in my own way. My book *Close to me . . . & Closer (The Language of Heaven)* is an attempt to contact death. It's a dialogue between a dead father and his daughter, in which he who in life was not intellectual or in the least well-educated or well-read attempts to tell her what "heaven" or "death" is like. He speaks his philosophy. He talks in prose, she responds in poems; he gets interested in poetry, she starts to talk in his stumbling manner. Their identities gradually merge, at least for a time, and she is able to enter, briefly, "god's room."

Writing *Close to me* made me happy, but then I became gloomy again and wrote the more feminine-epic-like book *Désamère*. *Désamère* is another work which focuses, at least partly anyway, on the dead soldier-brother; it more focuses on global ecological destruction. The problems it confronts have become bigger than those of sexism and war and poverty, since the future is seen as a negative, a desert. The poem is shorter perhaps because the problem is bigger . . . there's no one to kill, in this poem, because the machine of natural obliteration can't be stopped. However, as far as "feminine epic" goes as a form, I can say that the poem has a heroine, Amère who becomes Désamère, inspired by the dead French poet Robert Desnos, an oracular presence in this poem, to try to become something like an old-fashioned saint.

Thus she enters the heart of the desert and is tempted by a Satan, a glibly pro-Human psychologist, whom she does sleep with, but whose ultimate wiles—the mind-fuck into consorting with society, as it exists—she resists. Instead she writes visionary poetry before returning to what's left of human society to Help Out.

Since then. I still want to write an Epic. I know that some poems of Emily Dickinson's are as Epic as an Epic. Yet I want to write that large public poem. I want to discover a woman's voice that can encompass our true story existing on conscious and unconscious levels, in the literal present, witnessing more than one culture. We live in that total international multicultural natureless world. I may have to sound even more different from the traditional epic: I may have to sound funnier or more eccentric to do it properly this time. I mean I'm thinking about it again. I'm writing currently as a unified authorial "I" who Must Speak. There may not be a story next time I write Epic, there may be something more circuitous than recognized Time and Story, more winding, double-back. There will certainly be a Voice. I think it is essential that people like myself, and my brother, be heard: I can only do this by speaking out clearly. So perhaps I will write the epic of "my voice." That might be epic, something other than I'd thought might now be epic. A voice itself. A woman's voice. A woman's voice with access to the mystery of the dream.

# Acknowledgments

All quotations in "O'Hara in the Nineties" are taken from *The Collected Poems of Frank O'Hara* (New York: Knopf, 1979).

Books referred to in "Joanne Kyger's Poetry" include *All This Every Day* (Bolinas: Big Sky, 1975); *The Tapestry and the Web* (San Francisco: Four Seasons Foundation, 1965); *Places to Go* (Black Sparrow, 1970); *Just Space, Poems 1979–1989* (Santa Barbara, CA, and Ann Arbor, MI: Black Sparrow, 1991); and *The Wonderful Focus of You* (Calais, VT: Z Press, 1980), all by Joanne Kyger.

Books and magazines referred to in "Lorenzo Thomas: A Private Public Space" include *Chances Are Few*, by Lorenzo Thomas (Berkeley: Blue Wind Press, 1979); *The Bathers*, by Lorenzo Thomas (Berkeley: Reed & Cannon Communications, 1981); *From the Other Side of the Century: A New American Poetry*, edited by Douglas Messerli (Los Angeles: Sun & Moon Press, 1994); *Disembodied Poetics: Annals of the Jack Kerouac School*, edited by Anne Waldman and Andrew Schelling (Albuquerque: University of New Mexico Press, 1994); and SCARLET, no. 2 (Fall 1990).

Books by Steve Carey include *AP* (New York: Archipelago Books, 1984); *The California Papers* (New York: United Artists, 1981); *Fleur-de-Lis* (San Francisco: Blue Suede Shoes VII, 1968); *Gentle Subsidy* (Bolinas: Big Sky, 1975); *The Lily of St. Marks* (New York: "C" Press, 1978); *Smith Going Backwards* (San Francisco: Cranium Press, 1968); and *20 Poems* (New York: Unimproved Editions Press, 1987).

"American Poetic Music at the Moment" quotes from the following books: *Joker, Joker, Deuce*, by Paul Beatty (New York: Penguin, 1994); *Selected Poems*, by Ted Berrigan (New York: Penguin,

1994); *The Complete Poems,* by Edwin Denby (New York: Random House, 1986); *The Quietist,* by Fanny Howe (Oakland: O Books, 1992); *Going On: Selected Poems 1958–1980,* by Joanne Kyger (New York: Dutton, 1983); *Not Me,* by Eileen Myles (New York: Semiotext(e), 1991); *Close to me . . . & Closer (The Language of Heaven)* and *Désamère,* by Alice Notley (Oakland: O Books, 1995); *The Descent of Alette,* by Alice Notley (New York: Penguin, 1996); *Selected Poems of Alice Notley* (Hoboken: Talisman House Publishers, 1993); *Woven Stone,* by Simon J. Ortiz (Tucson and London: University of Arizona Press, 1992); *Defoe,* by Leslie Scalapino (Los Angeles: Sun & Moon Press, 1994); and *The Bathers,* by Lorenzo Thomas (Berkeley: Reed & Cannon Communications, 1981).

"Thinking and Poetry" quotes from the following books: *New & Selected Poems,* by Ron Padgett (Boston: David R. Godine, 1995); *Progress* by Barrett Watten (New York: Roof Books, 1985); *Waltzing Matilda* by Alice Notley (Cambridge, MA: Faux Press, 2003); *The Complete Poems of Emily Dickinson* by Emily Dickinson (Boston and Toronto: Little, Brown and Company, 1960); *How to Write* by Getrude Stein (New York: Dover Publications, Inc., 1975).

Books and poems referred to in "The 'Feminine' Epic" include *The Descent of Alette; Close to me . . . & Closer (The Language of Heaven),* and *Désamère. Beginning with a Stain* is available in *The Scarlet Cabinet,* a compendium of books by Alice Notley and Douglas Oliver (New York: Scarlet Editions, 1992). "White Phosphorus" is available in the latter book, in the "Homer's Art" section, and also in *Selected Poems of Alice Notley.* For the Inanna story I use primarily *Inanna: Queen of Heaven and Earth,* by Diane Wolkstein and Samuel Noah Kramer (New York: Harper & Row, 1983).